W9-CZK-621

# NEXT-GENERATION MEDICAL TECHNOLOGY

# Genetics and Medicine

Toney Allman

ReferencePoint
Press®

San Diego, CA

© 2018 ReferencePoint Press, Inc.
Printed in the United States

**For more information, contact:**
ReferencePoint Press, Inc.
PO Box 27779
San Diego, CA 92198
www.ReferencePointPress.com

LIBRARY OF CONGRESS CATALOGING-IN-PUBLICATION DATA

Name: Allman, Toney.
Title: Genetics and Medicine/by Toney Allman.
Description: San Diego, CA: Publisher: ReferencePoint Press, Inc., 2018. |
   Series: Next-Generation Medical Technology series | Audience: Grade 9 to
   12. | Includes bibliographical references and index.
Identifiers: LCCN 2017036690 (print) | LCCN 2017038665 (ebook) | ISBN
   9781682823262 (eBook) | ISBN 9781682823255 (hardback)
Subjects: LCSH: Gene therapy—Juvenile literature. | Genetics—Juvenile
   literature.
Classification: LCC RB155.8 (ebook) | LCC RB155.8 .A455 2018 (print) | DDC
   615.8/95—dc23
LC record available at https://lccn.loc.gov/2017036690

# CONTENTS

# IMPORTANT EVENTS IN THE HISTORY OF GENETICS

**1982**
Genentech, the company founded by Herbert Boyer and Stanley Cohen, markets human insulin made with recombinant DNA technology.

**1959**
Jérôme Lejeune identifies trisomy 21 as the cause of Down syndrome.

**1864**
Working with pea plants, Gregor Mendel discovers the discrete units of inheritance, through which traits are passed from parent to offspring.

**1952**
Alfred Hershey and Martha Chase use viruses and bacteria to demonstrate that genes are made of deoxyribonucleic acid (DNA).

**1875    1900    1925    1950    1975**

**1911**
Studying fruit flies, Thomas Hunt Morgan determines that genes are carried by chromosomes.

**1953**
Francis H. Crick and James D. Watson, along with Rosalind Franklin and Maurice Wilkins, discover the double-helix structure of DNA.

**1983**
Scientists determine that Huntington's disease can be traced to a mutated gene.

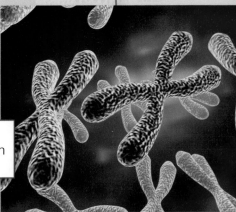

**1955**
Joe Hin Tjio determines that human cells have forty-six chromosomes.

4

**1990**
Doctors successfully perform the world's first gene therapy on four-year-old Ashanti DeSilva to correct her nonfunctioning immune system.

**2003**
The Human Genome Project is completed; the sequencing is estimated to be 99.99 percent accurate.

**2012**
Six-year-old Emily Whitehead becomes the first child to be treated for and cured of her leukemia with genetically engineered T cells—a method called CAR-T cell therapy.

**1999**
Jesse Gelsinger dies in a failed gene therapy trial; the event led to a major setback in the progress of gene therapy and resulted in the adoption of stringent standards for human trials.

**2007**
Doctors successfully employ gene therapy to give vision to a human patient with Leber's congenital amaurosis, a type of blindness.

**2016**
The European community approves Strimvelis as a gene therapy for children with adenosine deaminase severe combined immunodeficiency.

**1995**     **2000**     **2005**     **2010**     **2015**

**2006**
The first success in treating cancer with gene therapy targets advanced melanoma in humans, using genetically altered immune system cells.

**1997**
Researchers map the complete DNA sequence of the whole genome of the E. coli bacterium.

**2017**
Researchers at Necker Hospital for Sick Children in Paris, France, report curing a teenage boy of sickle cell disease using gene therapy.

**2001**
The US Food and Drug Administration approves the cancer drug Gleevec as a precision medicine treatment for people with chronic myelogenous leukemia.

# A Revolution in Medicine

In November 2016, seventy-nine-year-old Doralee Mortensen threw a party to celebrate a very important event. She had survived for twenty-five years after being diagnosed with chronic myelogenous leukemia (CML). She is now the longest-living CML patient in the world, but she is definitely not the last. CML is a kind of blood cancer characterized by the overgrowth of cancerous immature white blood cells. In 1991, when Mortensen was first diagnosed, CML was basically a death sentence. Mortensen remembers of that time, "I looked up all the statistics: 80 percent chance of dying in two years, 10 percent chance of dying within six months, 10 percent chance of living to 10 years. Nobody lived past 10 years. And there's no cure."[1] All doctors could do was to offer cancer treatments that might extend Mortensen's life by a few years.

## A New Way to Treat Cancer

Fortunately for Mortensen, standard chemotherapy treatment for her cancer did keep her alive for several years, but in 1998 her time was running out. That was when Dr. Brian J. Druker at Oregon Health and Science University selected her to participate in an experimental trial of a new drug. The drug, a pill known as imatinib and later marketed under the name Gleevec, had a remarkable effect. It reversed Mortensen's CML, as it did for almost everyone else in the trial. For the thirty-one test subjects, the drug began working almost immediately to kill cancer cells. Even Druker found it hard to believe. He remembers, "I'm looking at this and thinking, 'This is amazing. We've never seen anything like this before.' These are people who'd been told to get their affairs in order. And now their blood counts are normal."[2] In most patients, the cancer cells vanished and never returned. Nevertheless, Druker cautiously waited to see if the astounding results would last. They did.

The CML patients in this beginning phase I trial were the first humans ever to try imatinib. Usually, a phase I trial simply tests an experimental drug's safety in humans. If the treatment is safe, the drug then goes through a larger phase II trial to determine efficacy and a still larger phase III trial. Only then do its manufacturers apply to the US Food and Drug Administration (FDA) for approval to sell the drug. But imatinib was so stunningly effective right away that Druker and Novartis (the drug company supporting his experiments) applied for a fast-track approval from the FDA. The FDA granted approval in 2001, the fastest any cancer treatment has ever been approved. The drug definitely could extend lives, even though no one knew if the effects would be permanent. By November 2002, however, Druker was able to tell Mortensen that she had just 1 percent cancerous cells left in her blood. She would survive for sure. Mortensen says, "So I called everybody that I knew. . . . We celebrated over lunch."[3]

Today imatinib (Gleevec) has saved the lives of thousands of people, and CML is no longer a death sentence. Researchers have determined that patients whose blood counts are normal after two years on Gleevec have the same life expectancy as normal people who never had cancer. Dr. Dan Longo of Harvard Medical School and deputy editor of the *New England Journal of Medicine* wrote an article titled, "Imatinib Changed Everything."[4]

**gene**

the basic unit of heredity that determines characteristics and traits

## Revolutionizing the Treatment of Disease

CML is caused by a malfunctioning gene, named BCR-ABL, that codes for an enzyme that stimulates the uncontrolled growth of white blood cells. Uncontrolled cell growth is the hallmark of all cancers. Druker's drug turns off the enzyme that causes CML. Imatinib is a specific treatment that targets the cause of a particular kind of cancer, and that is why the therapy is so successful. CML is unusual in that its cause is a single malfunctioning gene. Many more common cancers are more difficult to treat because

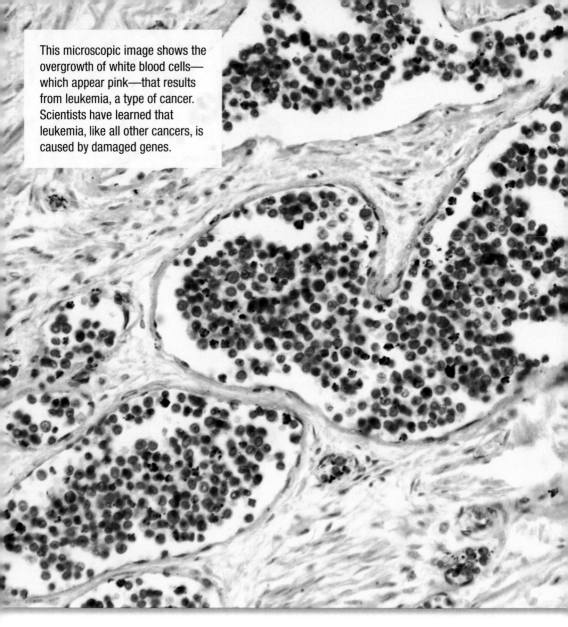

This microscopic image shows the overgrowth of white blood cells—which appear pink—that results from leukemia, a type of cancer. Scientists have learned that leukemia, like all other cancers, is caused by damaged genes.

the problem lies with multiple genes instead of a single gene. However, scientists now know that damaged genes are the cause of all cancers. The National Cancer Institute explains, "Cancer is a genetic disease—that is, cancer is caused by certain changes to genes that control the way our cells function, especially how they grow and divide."[5] The gene changes that enable a cancer to grow can be inherited, be acquired during a lifetime from environmental factors, or result from genetic errors that appear when a fetus is developing. But whatever the origin, that genetic change will not have to determine a person's fate anymore.

Recognizing the genetic cause of CML and then learning how to treat the result of the genetic problem has totally changed how the medical world conceives of cancer and develops targeted treatments for different types of cancers. Several gene-based cancer treatments have now been developed or are currently being researched. Furthermore, scientists are learning more and more about the genetic factors underlying all diseases, not just cancer. The ability to understand and manipulate the genes that lead to diseases and to alter genetic material for use in treatment has revolutionized medical treatment and health care in general. Medical scientists predict that these capabilities will completely transform the diagnosis, prevention, and treatment of many diseases in the near future.

**fetus**

the unborn, developing baby from two months after conception until birth

# CHAPTER 1

# Understanding Genes and DNA

For thousands of years, humankind has known that many traits are passed from parents to offspring. People saved the seeds from the strongest, most fruitful plants to replant the next season in the hope of a more bountiful harvest. They bred the fastest mare to the fastest stallion because they wanted to produce the fastest future racehorses. They selected the dogs born with curly tails or smaller sizes to breed for those traits and chose the puppies born with those characteristics to breed again. In this way domesticated animals and plants developed over time. No one, however, understood how inheritance worked, how traits were passed on, or why breeding programs succeeded or failed.

Not until the monk Gregor Mendel conducted studies of pea plants in his monastery garden did the rules of inheritance begin to make sense. In experiments conducted between 1856 and 1863, Mendel determined that at least some traits (such as tall and short) were inherited in plants from their parent plants and that he could describe mathematically the chances that a plant would inherit a particular trait. He was able to establish simple rules of inheritance that applied to all the generations of his peas. Mendel's discoveries were published in 1864, but science did not recognize the importance of his research until the beginning of the twentieth century.

In 1906 William Bateson coined the word *genetics* to describe the study of inheritance that Mendel had undertaken. Three years later Danish botanist Wilhelm Johannsen first used the term *genes* to identify the unknown "particles" that Mendel assumed carried an organism's traits. Bateson, Johannsen, and other early researchers worked to understand the molecules in living cells that were responsible for the inherited traits that Mendel had observed and scientists were now replicating. As a result, knowledge of genetics exploded, and today genetics continues to be one of the most rapidly advancing fields of study in the world.

**inheritance**

the transmission of genetic qualities from parents to offspring

## In the Nucleus of a Cell

The secret to inheritance lies hidden inside almost every cell in the body of every living thing. Cells are the body's building blocks, and each cell is a living, complex factory that manufactures proteins. Proteins do the work of the body. A red blood cell, for example, makes the protein hemoglobin that carries oxygen to all the cells of the body. A beta cell in the pancreas makes the protein insulin, which controls the use of glucose (a simple sugar used for energy) in the body's cells. Each cell knows what protein to manufacture because of the chemical instructions it receives from the nucleus in the cell's center. The nucleus contains the spiraled coils of deoxyribonucleic acid (DNA). DNA is what carries the genetic instructions for every living thing. In humans, DNA is arranged into twenty-three pairs of chromosomes, one of each pair inherited from each parent. Chromosomes carry genetic information in the form of genes. Genes are specific strings of DNA that are units of inheritance and code for specific proteins. These genes determine how the cells operate.

**karyotype**

a representation of the appearance, size, number, and shape of the chromosomes in an individual body

Different chromosomes contain different numbers of genes. In a photograph of human chromosomes—called a karyotype—the pairs of chromosomes are arranged according to size and numbered from 1 to 23. The biggest chromosome is chromosome 1, and it contains about eight thousand genes. The smallest chromosome is chromosome 21, containing only about three hundred genes. (The University of Leicester in the United Kingdom explains, "Chromosome 22 should be the smallest, but the scientists made a mistake when they first numbered them!"[6]) Chromosome pair 23 is special. The two chromosomes are of different sizes and are the sex chromosomes that determine whether the person is male or female. The larger X chromosome is female, and the smaller Y is male. If the pair is XX, the person is female, and if the chromosome pair is XY, he is male.

Altogether, humans have about twenty thousand to twenty-five thousand genes, but only about 3 percent of the DNA coiled in the chromosomes carries genes. The rest of the DNA strand

Austrian monk Gregor Mendel (pictured) conducted experiments with pea plants that proved that the characteristics of living things are inherited from their parents. Published in 1864, Mendel's work went largely unrecognized in the scientific community until the early twentieth century.

is something of a mystery. At one time, scientists thought this DNA had no function, but today, they believe it is involved in controlling the genes and how they function. It is the genes, however, that are the basic units of inheritance and the foundation of genetics.

## How Genes Determine Traits

Genes, just like chromosomes, come in pairs. One gene comes from the father and one from the mother. When a gene determines a simple, single trait, such as eye color or the height of a pea plant, the way it works is easy to understand using Mendel's rules. Of that pair of genes, one will be dominant—that is, always expressed—over the other. For example, if a baby—say, a girl—inherits one blue-eyed gene from her mother and one brown-eyed gene from her father, the baby will have brown eyes. That is because the gene for brown eyes is dominant and the gene for blue eyes recessive. The baby will carry the gene for blue all her life, but it will never be expressed, even though that gene might be passed on to her own children someday.

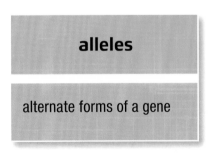

**expressed**

converted into instructions for making proteins

Variants of genes are common for many traits. Such variants are called alleles. When that baby girl grows up, she may have children with a man who also carries one blue eye allele and one brown. He will have brown eyes, too, but according to Mendelian rules, each of their offspring will have a 25 percent chance of having blue eyes. Since each parent passes along one gene for eye color, the offspring's gene pair may be two brown alleles, brown from mother and blue from father, or blue from mother and brown from father. In all these cases (75 percent), the resulting baby will have brown eyes. But if each parent passes along the blue eye alleles, the baby will have the two recessive genes, and the blue eye trait will be expressed.

**alleles**

alternate forms of a gene

## Genes and Inherited Disease

Some inherited diseases work in this simple way, too. Cystic fibrosis (CF), for example, is an inherited autosomal recessive disease. This means that the gene that causes the disease is on one of the twenty-two chromosome pairs not related to sex determination and is recessive, not dominant. CF causes a thick, sticky mucus buildup that damages the lungs and digestive system. It can be inherited only if both parents are carriers of the CF gene. In other words, each parent has two genes—one normal and the other causing the disease. Because the gene is recessive, it is never expressed in the parent; the normal gene is dominant and the parent healthy. However, each child born to parents who both carry the recessive gene will have a 25 percent chance of inheriting both recessive genes and thus having CF.

In 1989 scientists identified the CFTR gene on chromosome 7 that is defective and causes CF. Before that time, parents had no way of knowing they were carriers of CF unless they had a child with the disease. All doctors could do, after the child was born and diagnosed, was explain to the parents that CF was genetic and that there was a 25 percent risk that any future children would be born with the same disease. Several other autosomal recessive disorders, such as Tay-Sachs and sickle cell disease, are inherited in the same way as CF because of different defective genes. Today many of these genes have been identified, and parents can be tested to see if they are carriers before they decide to have children.

A few inherited genetic diseases are autosomal dominant. This means that if a child inherits even one defective gene from a parent's gene pair, he or she will have the disease. The gene dominates the normal gene inherited from the other parent. Usually, the parent who passed on the gene has the disease, too. Huntington's disease is an example of an autosomal dominant disorder. It is a progressive and fatal brain disease, but the symptoms do not appear until the affected person is in his or her thirties or forties, and so the individual's children are often born before the first symptoms begin.

Achondroplasia, a kind of dwarfism, also can be inherited as an autosomal dominant disorder. A person with an autosomal dominant condition has a 50 percent risk of passing on that gene

# Sex-Linked Disorders

Genetic mutations and disorders can occur on the sex-determining chromosome 23, as well as on the other twenty-two autosomal chromosomes. Usually, these genetic errors are carried on the larger X chromosome and are recessive. Since the mother has two X chromosomes, she would not have the disease even if she carried the problematic chromosome. Her normal X chromosome is dominant over the damaged X chromosome. If the mother gives birth to a boy and passes her damaged chromosome to him, however, he will develop the disease because, as a male, he has only one X chromosome. Boys are most likely to be affected by sex-linked recessive diseases; girls are rarely affected. Hemophilia, for example, is a sex-linked recessive disease that causes abnormal bleeding. About one in every seventy-five hundred males is born with hemophilia, but only one in 25 million females has the disease. Duchenne muscular dystrophy is another sex-linked recessive disease that almost always affects boys. Color blindness is also inherited as a sex-linked disorder, passed on by the mother's damaged X chromosome. The only way that a girl can be born with a recessive X-linked disorder is if her father has the disease and her mother is a carrier, and that circumstance is unlikely, given that most such disorders are rare in the population.

to any offspring. This inheritance pattern is why two people with achondroplasia can have children of average height. Dr. Barry Starr of Stanford University explains:

> Now imagine two parents with dwarfism. Which copy of a gene we get from our parents is random. So for this discussion, each parent [with one dwarfism gene each] has a 50-50 shot of passing down a copy that does not lead to dwarfism.
>
> What this means is that 25% of the time, the child will get a copy of the average height gene from both parents. The result will be a child of average height. . . . Two parents with dwarfism can have a child of average height because the parents are carriers of that trait.[7]

The DNA instructions of a gene determine common variants, such as eye color, and also uncommon traits, such as dwarfism or having CF.

# How Autosomal Recessive Disorders Are Inherited

Some diseases are the result of genetic traits that are passed from parents to children. Cystic fibrosis is one such disease. It is an autosomal recessive disorder. This means that each parent carries a recessive gene for the disorder. Since their normal genes are dominant, neither parent is affected by the disorder. They are carriers. However, any offspring who inherits the recessive gene from both parents will have the disorder. As the diagram shows, each child has a 25 percent chance of inheriting two normal genes and being healthy, a 50 percent chance of inheriting one normal gene and one mutated gene and being a carrier, and a 25 percent chance of inheriting both recessive genes and having the disorder.

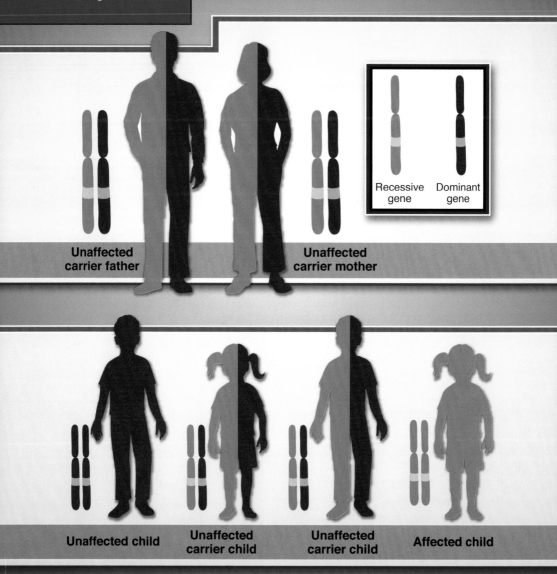

Recessive gene    Dominant gene

Unaffected carrier father

Unaffected carrier mother

Unaffected child

Unaffected carrier child

Unaffected carrier child

Affected child

Source: Mayo Clinic, "Autosomal Recessive Inheritance Pattern."
www.mayoclinic.org/autosomal-recessive-inheritance-pattern/img-20007457.

## The DNA Code of the Gene

The DNA structure was discovered in 1953 by scientists James D. Watson, Francis H. Crick, Maurice Wilkins, and Rosalind Franklin. That structure carries genetic instructions that tell the cells how to function. In each chromosome, there are two strands of DNA arranged in a twisted, coiling ladder. Each rung is made up of a pair of nitrogen bases, usually expressed in scientific code by the first letter of their names. These bases are adenine (A), thymine (T), guanine (G), and cytosine (C), and they bond in specific ways. Adenine joins only with thymine to make a base or rung of the ladder, and cytosine joins only with guanine.

In a human body, inside the nucleus of every cell are about 3 billion base pairs that have existed since the person was just a single cell, a fertilized egg called a zygote, that grew by cell division into an embryo and then a fetus and finally a newborn baby with trillions of cells. Each cell carries the complete DNA code in its nucleus, but most of the coded instructions are turned off in each cell. Every cell uses only the pertinent instructions that spell out the code for the protein that the cell must produce in order to function properly. The "words," or instructions, are spelled out by the specific ordering of groups of three bases along the strands— for example, CTG. DNA writes out the instructions, but it does not actually make the proteins. Instead, it passes the information to ribonucleic acid (RNA), also in groups of three bases. RNA is the cell's messenger and transfer system. It tells the cell what protein to manufacture. Geneticist Ricki Lewis explains, "Genetic information 'flows' from DNA (gene) to RNA to protein, and it is the protein that imparts the trait."[8]

## Mutations

Most of the time, cells function perfectly, but sometimes there are mistakes in the DNA code. A change in a gene and its DNA coding is called a mutation. A mutation can be inherited, arise spontaneously during the cell copying and division that occurs as an embryo is growing, or occur from environmental factors (such as smoking) that may damage a gene during a person's lifetime. Scientists say that DNA is like a giant book, and mutations are typographical errors. Everyone has such mistakes in their DNA codes. Geneticist Steven Monroe Lipkin says, "We each carry more than one hundred potential mutations in one gene or another."[9] Most of the time, such mutations do no harm. Genes function as a complicated network, and often they can compensate for a coding error. Mutations can even be beneficial because they help animals or species gain traits that help them survive. Sometimes, however, mutations lead to genetic diseases or disabilities, as they do with autosomal recessive and dominant disorders.

British chemist Jim Clark gives an example of the DNA mutation that is the cause of sickle cell disease, a condition in which red blood cells are stiff and crescent-shaped instead of round. The change in shape makes the cells sticky, which leads to pain and organ damage. Clark explains, "The affected part of the gene should read: . . . CTGACTCCT**GAG**GAGAAGTCT. . . . What it actually reads in someone suffering from sickle cell [disease] is: . . . CTGACTCCT**GTG**GAGAAGTCT. . . ."[10] The one tiny change in the single three-letter grouping that is boldfaced in the sequence changes how the protein hemoglobin functions and alters the shape of red blood cells.

Finding the typographical errors in DNA that affect how a gene functions can be extremely difficult. Genes can have different kinds of errors that might lead to a disease. The CFTR gene, for instance, can have more than seventeen hundred mutations in DNA coding that cause CF. Some of these mutations are quite rare, and others are more common. In CF and in other diseases, the mutations can involve a substitution of a nitrogen base (as with sickle cell disease), an omission of bases, or an addition of bases. Furthermore, many kinds of diseases, such as cancer, heart disease, or diabetes, are not the result of a single gene but of multiple genetic errors and variants occurring together. In all these circumstances, understanding normal DNA sequences is necessary if medical scientists are to identify improper sequencing.

## The Human Genome

The tool that researchers use to explore variations and errors in DNA coding and genes is the entire sequence of the human genome, or the complete set of the roughly 3 billion base pair configurations with the DNA of humans. After thirteen years of work, the human genome was completely mapped in 2003 by the Human Genome Project—a worldwide scientific effort to list every chemical letter of the bases on the DNA ladder in its exact order and to name and locate every gene in each chromosome and discover the function of every gene. Scientists now know the structure and sequence of the human genome and can identify most genes, but they have not yet found every gene. Genes are just base pair sequences on the DNA ladder, and identifying where each starts and stops is not easy. That is why the number of genes in humans is always reported as an estimate. Scientists

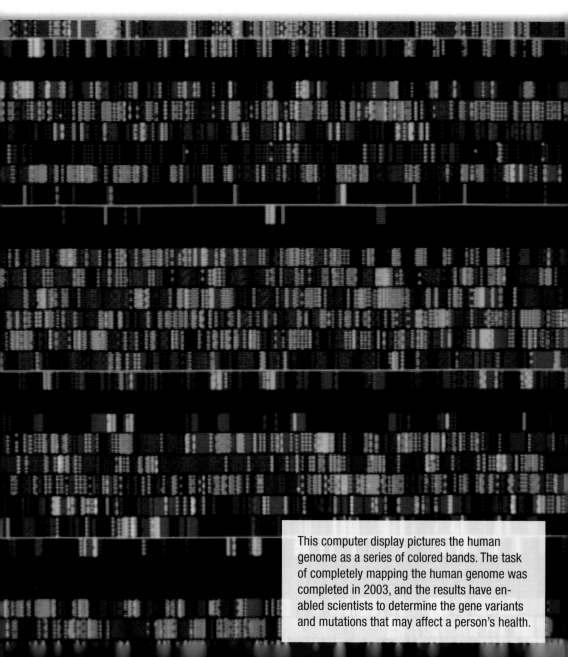

This computer display pictures the human genome as a series of colored bands. The task of completely mapping the human genome was completed in 2003, and the results have enabled scientists to determine the gene variants and mutations that may affect a person's health.

also do not know the functions of all the genes or how the DNA that does not code for proteins affects and regulates the genes.

Mapping and sequencing the first human genome was a massive, time-consuming, and hugely expensive endeavor. The project, which extended from 1990 to 2003, cost more than $2 billion and involved research groups around the world. Now, with advances in DNA sequencing technology and computerized analysis, any individual's personal genome can be mapped and compared to the average human genome for less than $1,500. Analyzing just part of the genome—for instance, to look for a specific gene mutation—is even easier. Researchers often can identify a gene suspected of causing disease in a matter of days. And gene sequencing is offered by commercial enterprises as well as by academic and medical services. Every individual's genome is unique, and mapping that genome can provide the information about that person's whole DNA sequence and his or her complete set of genes. It enables scientists to determine the gene

## A Unique Individual

When the human egg and sperm cells unite to form the fertilized egg called a zygote, each has only half the chromosomes of other cells. Both egg and sperm cells are formed from a parent cell in the mother and father. First each parent cell divides into two identical cells. Then each chromosome lines up beside its double and, in a mixing and matching process, exchanges DNA with the other. This process ensures that the genetic information in each sex cell is unique. Next the sex cell undergoes meiosis. During meiosis, the sex cell divides twice and forms four daughter cells, each with only half the chromosomes of the original cell. Now each sperm or egg cell has only twenty-three chromosomes, not forty-six. When sperm and egg unite, the twenty-three chromosomes in each cell fuse in the new zygote, which now has the full complement of forty-six chromosomes. Half of the zygote's genetic information comes from the mother and half from the father. The zygote grows through mitosis, or cell division, into two, then four, then eight, then sixteen cells, and so on, with each cell containing identical chromosomes that carry information unique to that individual. The zygote continues to grow and becomes an embryo as the cells multiply, group together to form layers, and specialize into all the organs of a human being with DNA that is not quite identical to any other human ever conceived.

variants and mutations that may affect that person's health, identify the cause of a disease, or determine what kinds of treatment might work best to fight a disease.

## Medicine and the Genome

Much is left to learn about DNA, genes, and the science of genomics. However, the National Institutes of Health (NIH) predicts, "Individualized analysis based on each person's genome will lead to a powerful form of preventive, personalized and preemptive medicine. By tailoring recommendations to each person's DNA, health care professionals will be able to work with individuals to focus efforts on the specific strategies—from diet to high-tech medical surveillance—that are most likely to maintain health for that particular individual."[11] Already, this knowledge is changing the face of medicine.

# CHAPTER 2

# Personalized Medicine

In 2013 actress Angelina Jolie revealed to the public that she had undergone a double mastectomy (surgical removal of both breasts) to prevent getting breast cancer in the future. Jolie took this radical step because she had her genome sequenced and discovered that she carried an inherited gene mutation that dramatically increased her risk of developing breast cancer. Her mother, grandmother, and an aunt had all died of breast or cervical cancer. With the cells of her breasts gone, she reduced the risk of developing breast cancer herself by 90 percent. Jolie wrote about her decision, "I choose not to keep my story private because there are many women who do not know that they might be living under the shadow of cancer. It is my hope that they, too, will be able to get gene tested, and that if they have a high risk they, too, will know that they have strong options."[12]

## How Personalized Medicine Works

Personalized medicine is a type of medical care that uses a person's genetic profile to prevent, diagnose, and treat disease. It is targeted therapy that precisely attacks or treats a medical problem in an individual rather than depending on one standard treatment for everyone. This kind of precision medicine is exemplified by Jolie's medical diagnosis and subsequent preventive treatment. Reviewing her genetic profile, doctors determined she was at risk for a disease and consulted with her to tailor treatment decisions to her particular situation.

Most cases of breast cancer are not inherited. Medical researchers believe that most breast cancers are caused by mutations in multiple genes in breast cells that a person slowly acquires during a lifetime. Such acquired mutations may arise from

lifestyles, nutritional factors, hormonal changes, or other environmental factors, but scientists do not know how or why they cause
cells to become cancerous. About 5 percent to 10 percent of
breast cancers, however, are inherited. Half of these cancers are
caused by two gene mutations, known as BRCA1 and BRCA2.
Both of these genetic mutations are inherited in an autosomal
dominant pattern. That means that just one of these genes, inherited from either parent, greatly increases the chance of developing breast cancer.

The actress Angelina Jolie (right) is pictured with
her mother, who died of cancer. When genetic tests
revealed that Jolie had inherited a gene mutation
that dramatically increased her own risk of
developing breast cancer, she opted for a double
mastectomy that reduced this risk by 90 percent.

When Jolie underwent genetic testing, she might have discovered that she had no genetic mutations that increased her risk of breast cancer. In that case her personalized medical diagnosis would have let her know that her chance of developing breast cancer during her lifetime was only about 12.4 percent—the same as for most women. Jolie, however, learned that she does carry the BRCA1 mutation and that her risk of getting breast cancer in the future was 87 percent. No medical treatment can cure inherited breast cancer yet, but Jolie did have options for lowering her risks. Some people with the BRCA1 and BRCA2 mutations opt for a wait-and-see approach that includes increased frequency of screening for any signs of breast cancer. Some also take medications that lower the risk that cancer will begin to grow. Some, like Jolie, choose to have their breasts removed so that the cells where the cancer could grow are gone and the risk of breast cancer is almost eliminated.

## How Doctors and Patients Use Genetic Information

Personalized medicine provided Jolie with information, but it could not make the decision for her about what to do. Only she could make that decision. In 2015 she also chose to have her ovaries

## A Precision Attack on a Virus

Hepatitis C is a liver disease caused by a virus. It can cause serious liver damage, liver cancer, liver failure, and death if it goes untreated. Scientists have identified the DNA of the hepatitis C virus and determined that there are six different genotypes (genetic makeups). Using this precise knowledge of viral DNA, researchers were able to develop antiviral drugs to target and kill different strains of the hepatitis C viruses. Viruses have to reproduce inside human cells in order to survive, and antiviral drugs work by blocking the part of the virus that controls reproduction. The first antiviral drug for hepatitis C was named sofosbuvir. It was approved by the FDA in 2013 and targeted the genotypes 1, 2, 3, and 4. A second drug, called ledipasvir, was approved in 2014 and worked against types 1, 4, 5, and 6. In 2016 a drug that combines both antiviral treatments was introduced. This drug became the first to treat and stop reproduction in all six viral genotypes. By 2017 the combination drugs were also approved as safe for use in adolescents aged twelve to seventeen who suffer with chronic hepatitis C infections. Hepatitis C is no longer a killer disease, and at least 98 percent of those treated with the precision antiviral drugs are cured.

and fallopian tubes removed to reduce the risk of ovarian cancer, which is increased by the mutated BRCA1 gene, too. Jolie says, "It is not easy to make these decisions. But it is possible to take control and tackle head-on any health issue. You can seek advice, learn about the options and make choices that are right for you. Knowledge is power."[13]

Jolie was tested for her mutated gene because she was considered a high-risk patient. Family members had died of cancer at relatively young ages, and this family history suggested that she might develop an inherited form of the disease. But many in the medical community worry that such genetic testing will be overused or unnecessarily burden women with too much fear. After Jolie went public with her story in 2013, researchers at Harvard Medical School reported that genetic testing for the BRCA1 and BRCA2 mutations increased by 64 percent in just three weeks, as frightened people sought the testing for themselves. Most of them, however, tested negative for the mutations.

Doctors say that raising awareness is beneficial, and they want high-risk patients to be tested. But at the same time, they do not want excessive testing and stress for people who do not need it. And Harvard Medical School doctor Mark Boguski adds, "The negative effect of that disclosure is the women who went and had these tests, which came back negative now have a false sense of security that they weren't going to develop breast cancer—which is totally wrong."[14] All these women still have the 12.4 percent risk of getting a noninherited form of breast cancer sometime in their lives and still need to get regular checkups. Nevertheless, almost all doctors believe that Jolie performed a great public service in raising awareness about inherited breast cancer. She may have saved many lives by sharing her story, and she has been a wonderful example of how personalized medicine can benefit the minority of people with inherited faulty genes.

## Genetic Diagnosis and Treatment

Doctors are just beginning to realize the value of personalized medicine, and there is still much to be learned about genetics and disease. Physicians have always known that some diseases were more common in certain families than others. The medical world has long recognized that standard treatments, whether for cancers or other diseases, worked better for some people than others. But until recently, no one understood why. Now, with genomic testing, medical researchers are learning more and more about the genetic variants that can lead to disease and the many genetic ways that disease can arise. And they are finding better ways to treat those diseases within individuals.

Regarding CF, for instance, with its many different CFTR mutations, medical researchers have discovered a way to correct the functioning of the defective protein that is produced through certain coding errors. The drug ivacaftor increases the protein's activity and improves lung function in cases involving thirty-three of the CFTR mutations. Dr. Preston W. Campbell, president of the Cystic Fibrosis Foundation, says that ivacaftor can change the lives of young CF patients. He explains that it could mean "a life free from the severe and progressive complications associated with cystic fibrosis."[15] Ivacaftor is an example of personalized medicine that precisely targets the underlying genetic cause of a disease with a successful treatment, but it works only for those CF patients with thirty-three of the seventeen hundred possible mutations that cause the disease. And those mutations account for only about 10 percent of patients with CF. For the other 90 percent, successful precision treatment remains elusive despite ongoing research.

## A Project to Expand Genetic Knowledge

The more that researchers can uncover the genetic variants that cause disease and learn how those mutations result in the proteins that function incorrectly, the more they will be able to apply precision medicine to new treatments. Understanding genomes and why an individual's risks increase for specific diseases will someday make personalized medicine available to everyone. At least, that is the hope and goal of the All of Us Research Program initiated by then-president Barack Obama in 2016. Directed by the NIH, the project aims to open up a new era of medicine by expanding precision prevention and treatment options for all diseases, not just known inherited diseases such as CF. The NIH explains, "Precision medicine is a revolutionary approach for disease prevention and treatment that takes into account individual differences in lifestyle, environment, and biology [genetics]. While some advances in precision medicine have been made, the prac-

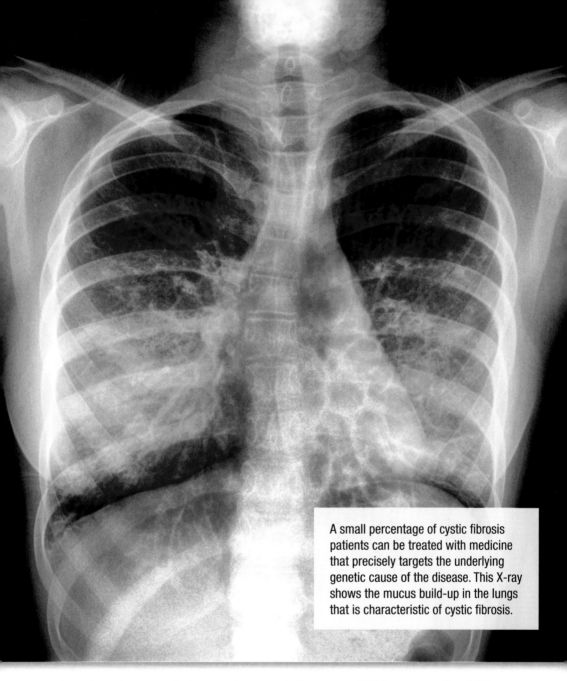

A small percentage of cystic fibrosis patients can be treated with medicine that precisely targets the underlying genetic cause of the disease. This X-ray shows the mucus build-up in the lungs that is characteristic of cystic fibrosis.

tice is not currently in use for most diseases."[16] However, the NIH hopes that will change.

The first major step in the All of Us Research Program is to collect medical information, including individual genomes, from 1 million or more US volunteers. Researchers will be able to use this information to study the ways genomes and environmental factors may interact and influence health and disease.

People across the country will be invited to join the program in 2018. As the program continues, individual volunteers will be given information about their own health and kept updated on the research findings, but the NIH promises that individual privacy will be respected, and no personal identifying information will be shared without permission. The NIH knows it could be years before the variables that lead to different diseases will be known and even longer before individualized treatments are developed. But most researchers agree that the data collected in such a large project will make understanding of disease processes and advances in personalized medicine proceed at a rapid pace.

## Personalized Medicine and Cancer Treatment

Personalized medicine has achieved the most promising success in cancer treatments. There are many kinds of cancer, but essentially all cancers are diseases in which certain cells begin to multiply through cell division and do not stop. The cells divide so rapidly that they can form a mass called a tumor, spread into body areas where they crowd out other normal cells, fail to die as old cells are supposed to do, and steal nutrition and oxygen from normal cells. The body has many genes that control cell division by turning the process on and off when needed. Scientists call these genes proto-oncogenes, and when something goes wrong with proto-oncogenes, cancer can arise. The American Cancer Society explains:

**proto-oncogene**

a gene that codes for a protein that regulates cell growth; when a proto-oncogene mutates, it may become an oncogene

> Proto-oncogenes are genes that normally help cells grow. When a proto-oncogene mutates (changes) or there are too many copies of it, it becomes a "bad" gene that can stay turned on or activated when it's not supposed to be. When this happens, the cell grows out of control and makes more cells that grow out of control. This can lead to cancer. This bad gene is called an oncogene.[17]

Oncogenes can turn normal cells into cancer cells. Other mutated genes that contribute to cancer are called tumor suppressor genes. These genes are supposed to slow down cell division and signal damaged and defective cells to die. When tumor suppressor genes do not work correctly, cells can grow out of control.

In 2006 the NIH began The Cancer Genome Atlas (TCGA) with the goal of mapping the genomes of cancerous cells for many different kinds of cancer. Ultimately, medical researchers use this genetic information to precisely diagnose and treat each patient's particular cancer. The TCGA explains, "Cancer is a disease of the genome and as more is learned about cancer tumors, the more we are finding that each tumor has its own set of genetic changes. Understanding the genetic changes that are in cancer cells is

## oncogene

a gene that has mutated such that it may cause the growth of cancer cells (*onco* is Latin for "tumor" or "malignancy")

## Saving Nicole

In 2015 Nicole Saldivar was sixteen years old when she was diagnosed with glioblastoma, a fast-growing brain cancer that is difficult to treat. Most people with glioblastoma die within about two years, even with surgery to remove the tumor, radiation therapy, and standard chemotherapy treatments. As the tumor grew, Nicole lost her ability to talk and walk. Then Nicole's parents took her to see Dr. Santosh Kesari of the John Wayne Cancer Institute in California. Kesari mapped the genome of Nicole's brain tumor and made an important discovery. He recalls, "She had a mutation of the P13K gene, one of the oncogenes for glioblastoma." That information gave Kesari an idea of how to treat Nicole's cancer. He explains, "We knew that a medication called everolimus is approved for this mutation in breast cancer and renal [kidney] cancer, so we believed it could work for her glioblastoma." Nicole was the first person ever to try this treatment for brain cancer, and it worked. After two months, her tumor had shrunk by 50 percent, and after a year it was 93 percent gone. By the spring of 2017, Nicole was talking again and getting therapy to regain her physical abilities. She says, "I can't wait to ride a bike and run again." Kesari says, "Nicole shows what precision medicine can do."

Quoted in Travis Marshall, "Precision Medicine Tailors Treatment to the Patient's Unique Biological Makeup," *Innovations*, Spring 2017, pp. 23, 24.

leading to more effective treatment strategies that are tailored to the genetic profile of each patient's cancer."[18] The TCGA, along with other cancer genome projects that grew out of its mapping, has identified the genomic types of dozens of cancers and revealed the pathways and mechanisms by which these cancers grow and spread. Already, this knowledge has led to lifesaving precision cancer treatments.

## Precisely and Successfully Treated

Teri Pollastro, for example, has been living with metastatic breast cancer since she was first diagnosed in 1999. Metastatic cancer is cancer that has spread to other body organs and tissues. It can be hard to survive. When Pollastro was diagnosed, she received a mastectomy and thought she was cured, but the cancer came back and had spread by 2003. That was when doctors were able to check her cancer's genetic profile and determine that her cancer was due to a faulty gene called HER2. About 20 percent of women with breast cancer are positive for HER2, which causes cancer cells to make too much growth protein. This protein instructs the cancer cells to grow very rapidly. Knowing the type of breast cancer has allowed researchers to develop a treatment—a drug called trastuzumab, or Herceptin. Herceptin works by latching on to the HER2 protein and blocking its growth signals. It specifically targets these cancer cells and slows or stops their growth. Pollastro began treatment with six months of traditional chemotherapy (which kills all fast-growing cells) and Herceptin. She had to continue the Herceptin treatment for seven years because the cancer had spread to so many places in her body, but she continued to improve and heal. The cancer cells continued to die. Today, at age fifty-six, Pollastro shows no evidence of disease. She is not definitely cured, because she knows the cancer could come back, but she says, "The longer I go, the less worried I get."[19]

Personalized medicine, which allows targeted treatment of HER2 breast cancer, has vastly improved survival rates for women with this type of cancer. Since Pollastro was first treated,

**metastatic**

referring to the spread of cancer cells from the initial site of the disease to other parts of the body researchers have developed other drugs that block more and different growth signals than Herceptin alone does. Medical researchers are now combining these drugs and killing the cancer cells even more efficiently. Dr. C. Kent Osborne thinks that in the future, such precision treatments will completely cure cancers such as HER2 breast cancer. In 2017 he predicted:

> I think we are in the era of genomic medicine, or targeted therapies, where we identify a specific abnormality in a patient's tumor and have a drug that would target that abnormality. . . . I think that targeted therapy will be the only therapy that we need. . . . We may not need nonspecific poison like chemotherapy, at least for certain tumors. There are other tumors that chemotherapy is still very effective for and will be hard to get rid of. But I think there will be many patients that can be treated with targeted therapies alone—not only in breast cancer, but in other tumors as well.[20]

## Living with Lung Cancer

Another kind of cancer that is being treated with precision medicine is lung cancer. As of May 2016, Stephanie Dunn Haney had been living with lung cancer for nine years. When she was first diagnosed, she was treated with standard chemotherapy to kill the cancer cells, but no one expected her to survive more than two years. Dunn Haney had never smoked (the major cause of lung cancer), and she was relatively young at thirty-nine years old, but she did have a mutation in a gene known as the EGFR gene. So far, researchers have identified three genes—ALK, KRAS, and EGFR—that can lead to lung cancer. No targeted treatment is available for faulty KRAS genes, although researchers currently are testing treatments for this mutation. With faulty ALK and EGFR genes, however, drugs have been developed that help block the actions of the genes and stop cancer tumors from growing. EGFR mutations make cancer cells keep dividing and multiplying. Dunn Haney's doctor prescribed a targeted treatment for this mutation that blocks the EGFR signals to the cells.

The treatment worked for two years, but then Dunn Haney's cancer cells grew resistant to the treatment and started growing again. By this time medical research had advanced, so her doctors could test her cancer genome again for more information. Dunn Haney also had the ALK mutation, and she immediately switched to the drug that targets the defective ALK gene. The

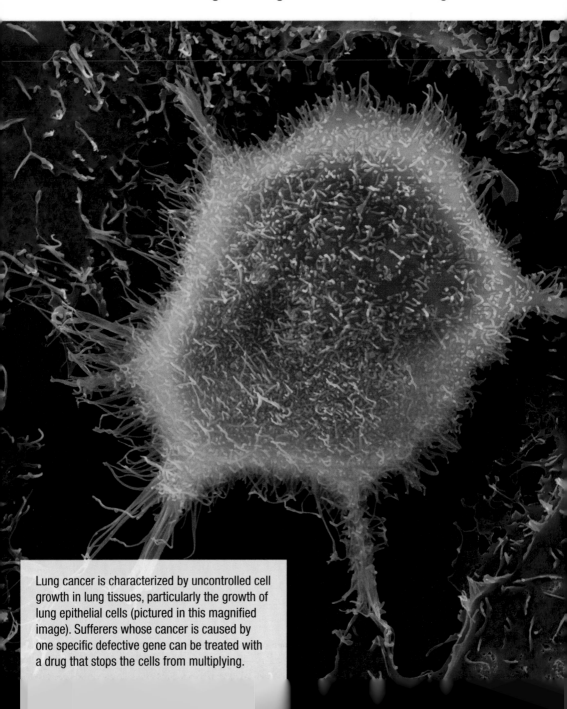

Lung cancer is characterized by uncontrolled cell growth in lung tissues, particularly the growth of lung epithelial cells (pictured in this magnified image). Sufferers whose cancer is caused by one specific defective gene can be treated with a drug that stops the cells from multiplying.

targeted drug acted like an off switch and stopped the cancer from growing. Dunn Haney has done extremely well, and her cancer cells are still not multiplying as long as she continues taking the drug. Her doctor says that even if the lung cancer cannot be

**resistant**

able to stop responding to a drug after being exposed to it

cured, it can be managed for many years. Dunn Haney herself says, "I have fairly normal energy levels and no one really knows I'm sick."[21]

Professor and geneticist Elaine Mardis says, "Lung cancer is a great example of personalized medicine."[22] The cancer's genetic profile is identifiable, the genetic mutations are discoverable, and targeted therapy can be used to precisely treat several lung cancer types. In the future, researchers are sure that many more cancers will become treatable with personalized medicine.

# CHAPTER 3

# Creating New Medicines

Viruses can make people very sick, and viruses can make a cancer tumor sick, too. A virus can make a cancer tumor so sick that it dies. Some cancers are quite vulnerable to infection by viruses, and some viruses prefer to infect cancer cells rather than healthy, normal cells. Melanoma, for example, is a kind of skin cancer that can spread rapidly, and it is particularly vulnerable to the herpes virus. In 2015 Randy Russell became one of a group of people testing a new treatment for melanoma. Russell had melanoma tumors spreading up and down his leg that doctors could not surgically remove and that were likely to kill him. In the trial treatment, each tumor was directly injected with a drug made from a genetically altered herpes virus. After the first injection, Russell's tumors began to shrink. After a series of injections, the tumors disappeared. Russell says, "I was absolutely amazed. It's like I never had [cancer], and I was ready to die."[23]

## An Oncolytic Virus to the Rescue

Like all viruses, the herpes virus is just a bundle of genetic material enclosed in a protein shell. Viruses infect the body and replicate by slipping inside cells and then tricking the cells into accepting the viral genetic instructions and coding for making more viruses. Once it has replicated many viruses, the cell splits open, spills the new viruses into the body to infect more cells, and dies. A virus that preferentially infects cancer cells in this way is called an oncolytic virus. To make the drug that helped Russell, researchers took advantage of the herpes virus's ability to alter a cell's genetic instructions and ultimately cause its death. First they made the virus harmless by snipping out the parts of the DNA sequence that cause sickness in people and allow it to enter healthy cells. Then they added a gene to the virus's DNA that codes for making a protein that attracts the white blood cells of the body's immune system to recognize and kill infected cells. The new drug was named Imlygic, and it works in two ways: It infects and kills cancer cells, and it stimulates the immune system.

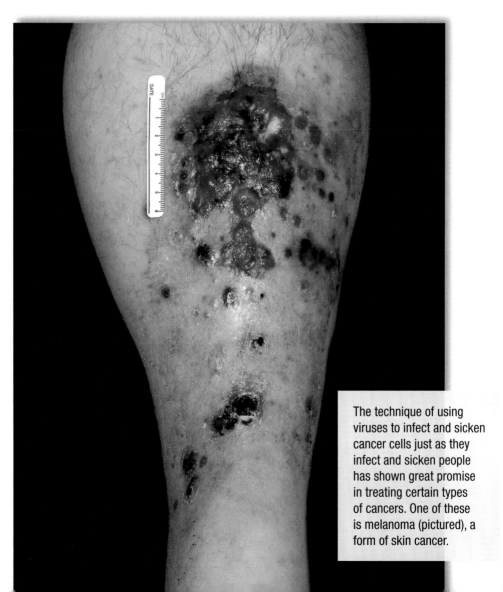

The technique of using viruses to infect and sicken cancer cells just as they infect and sicken people has shown great promise in treating certain types of cancers. One of these is melanoma (pictured), a form of skin cancer.

The immune system is the body's complex defense mechanism. It responds to any invading microorganism, such as a virus or bacterium, by mounting an attack against it. The immune system produces antibodies to signal that a full-out assault is necessary and launches white blood cells to attack and destroy the invader. Cancer cells, however, are able to hide from the immune system and continue to grow without signaling the immune system that something is wrong. Adding a gene to the herpes virus that helps the immune system recognize cancer gives an extra boost to the treatment by enlisting the body's own defenses to help conquer the cancer. Dr. Howard Kaufman, the leader of the research team that developed Imlygic, explains, "The thinking here is that one of the main jobs of T cells, which are white blood cells, is to circulate throughout the body and find viral infections, which should not be there. But we believe another one of their functions can be to look for and destroy cancer cells, which also should not be there."[24]

**antibodies**

proteins produced by the immune system to latch on to foreign materials in the body and render them harmless

Imlygic does not work for all patients with melanoma, especially those whose cancer has spread to other organs, but it is a lifesaver for many. In the people who responded to the treatment in the drug's trial, their risk of death was reduced by 95 percent, and almost half of the 2,116 injected tumors disappeared completely. Kaufman says, "It's remarkable. We are even seeing cures today in patients with very advanced melanoma."[25] In 2015 Imlygic became the world's first drug made from an oncolytic virus to be approved as a cancer treatment. But it is not the only genetically altered microorganism to be used in medicine. Bacteria, viruses, and yeasts have all been used to develop medicines through genetic engineering.

## Genetic Engineering and Bacteria

Genetic engineering involves deliberately changing the structure of the DNA or genome of an organism. An organism's genes can be modified or altered, or the genes from one species can be transferred to another. These genetically modified organisms (GMOs) can be used in medicine to create new vaccines and drugs for people. Many people disapprove of GMOs, especially when the organisms being modified are the plant foods that people eat. Examples of such plants are corn that is resistant to herbicides and thus can be sprayed with weed killers and remain healthy, and other crops that carry a gene from a bacterium that makes a toxin that kills insects feeding on the plant. People worry that genetically modified foods are unhealthy and dangerous for the natural environment. Most scientists disagree with this idea and consider GMOs to be safe, and they know that the medical uses of genetic engineering have proved their tremendous value.

The first genetic engineering success was the development of synthetic insulin for people with diabetes. In this instance, a biotechnology company named Genentech used a bacterium, *Escherichia coli* (E. coli), with the goal of cloning human insulin in such large quantities that it could meet the needs of the millions

## Healthy Tobacco

Mapp Biopharmaceutical is a company that makes drugs for infectious diseases. In 2016 the company announced that a small trial of a vaccine against the Ebola virus had achieved some success. Ebola is a deadly virus that killed more than eleven thousand people in Africa in an epidemic that began in 2014. Mapp's trial vaccine is made in a Kentucky greenhouse by injecting young tobacco plants with genetic instructions to make antibodies against the Ebola virus. The plants take the genetic coding into their cells and then manufacture the proteins that are Ebola antibodies. When the tobacco is harvested, chopped up, and purified into a liquid, the researchers at Mapp have a different kind of vaccine. Instead of injecting a killed virus to teach the immune system to make antibodies, doctors inject antibodies that have already been made into an infected patient.

The idea is to give this vaccine to Ebola patients who need antibody protection right away. The vaccine trial was conducted with seventy-two hospitalized Ebola patients in Africa. Half the patients were given regular hospital care, and the other half received the vaccine. The number of patients who died of Ebola was 40 percent lower for people treated with the vaccine than for those who did not receive it. Such a study is too small to prove that the vaccine is effective, but Ebola is so deadly that the FDA has asked Mapp to offer the vaccine on an experimental basis to patients if another epidemic occurs.

of people with diabetes. Diabetics had been using insulin to control their disease since 1922, but it was insulin purified from the pancreases of pigs and cows killed in slaughterhouses. This insulin saved lives, but it is not exactly the same as human insulin, and it often caused allergic reactions in people using it. Also, people's immune systems sometimes reacted to the animal insulin as if it were a foreign invader and produced antibodies to fight it. During the 1970s Herb Boyer and Stanley Cohen, who founded Genentech with businessman Bob Swanson, became determined to develop artificial human insulin that would solve these problems. The human genome was not yet known, but the insulin gene had been identified, and both Boyer and Cohen knew how to manipulate the DNA in bacteria.

A bacterium is a living, complex, single-celled microorganism. It has a nucleus with genes carrying the DNA coding that determines its functioning. But outside the nucleus, in the jelly-like substance of the cell, a bacterium has tiny structures called plasmids that do not occur in human cells. Plasmids are little loops of DNA that are duplicated every time a bacterium reproduces. Bacteria reproduce by cell division. In a good environment with enough food, a bacterial cell grows larger, makes exact copies of its DNA, and then divides, making two identical daughter cells. Each daughter cell can divide again, sometimes in as little as twenty minutes, and then those cells can divide again. With enough food and in a perfect environment (like a laboratory), a single bacterium can become a colony of 1 billion in ten hours through the process of cell division, with each bacterium an exact copy, or clone, of the first bacterium.

## Recombinant DNA Technology
The plasmids are exact copies, too, and plasmids are relatively easy for scientists to alter. That is what Boyer and Cohen did with E. coli bacteria in their laboratory. The E. coli that they used was a harmless strain that lives naturally in the human intestinal tract. The researchers chemically snipped the plasmid in the bacterium and then pasted in the human gene for making insulin. This process is called recombinant DNA technology, which recombines two separate pieces of DNA to form a new, artificial DNA sequence. The plasmids in the bacteria now carried the DNA code for making human insulin, and each bacterial daughter cell made

insulin as it was coded to do. The scientists at Genentech grew huge colonies of their genetically engineered bacteria, and then all they had to do was harvest and purify the insulin for human use. This synthetic human insulin made by bacteria was first sold to people in 1982.

Today everyone with diabetes who needs insulin uses synthetic human insulin produced either with bacteria or yeast cells through genetic engineering. The process is similar, although simpler and less expensive, to the one used by Boyer and Cohen. And insulin is no longer the only medicine manufactured in large quantities by E. coli bacteria.

Human growth hormone (HGH), for instance, is produced today using E. coli bacteria to help people with dwarfism. A hormone is a chemical substance naturally produced by the body

Dwarfism is a condition of short stature that results from a deficiency of human growth hormone (HGH). Genetic engineering has resulted in a method of producing synthetic HGH to treat this condition in affected children.

to regulate the activity of different cells or organs. HGH is a protein that helps control physical and mental growth, as well as the development of some body organs. When the body does not produce enough HGH, whether from genetic mutations or from damage to the pituitary gland where HGH is made, an individual may have dwarfism, or growth hormone deficiency. Today doctors can treat this condition by giving synthetic HGH to affected children and improving their physical growth, often enabling the child to achieve average height. Synthetic HGH is made by inserting the HGH gene and its DNA sequence into the plasmids of E. coli bacteria. Colonies of these genetically engineered bacteria manufacture plentiful HGH hormone that can be used for medical treatment. Other medical treatments developed from recombinant DNA technology include making a blood-clotting factor for people with hemophilia (a bleeding disorder) and laboratory production of interferons (proteins that stimulate the immune system) to fight the growth of some cancer cells and prevent the growth of some viruses.

## Vaccines and Preventing Disease

Scientists are also using genetically altered microorganisms to develop new vaccines. Vaccines are used to prevent disease. Typically, vaccines are designed in several different ways. Some are live, but much weakened, versions of the virus that causes the disease (such as chicken pox or measles). Some are killed viruses or bacteria that cause disease (like the rabies or polio vaccines). Other vaccines are called subunit vaccines. They contain only the pieces of the microorganism—called antigens—that the immune system uses to recognize a foreign invader. Subunit vaccines have been developed for influenza and pertussis (whooping cough). With all these vaccine types, the immune system responds as if the live, dangerous, disease-causing microorganism has attacked the body. The immune system's B cells—a type of white blood cell—react to the vaccine injection by producing antibodies that latch on to the antigens and signal other white blood cells called helper

**antigens**

any foreign molecules that produce an immune system response

T cells and killer T cells to destroy the infection. Once these disease-specific antibodies are produced, the immune system does not forget the disease. It makes memory B cells and memory T cells that linger in the immune system, ready to attack again the instant the body is exposed to that infection. That is how vaccines make people immune to many diseases and protect them from ever acquiring the actual disease.

Typical vaccines are powerful protections from disease, but they do have some disadvantages. Weakened live vaccines, for instance, could mutate and cause the actual disease. Killed vaccines are safe but provoke a weak immune system response that may not fully protect every person from disease. Identifying all the important antigens to make a subunit vaccine can be difficult and time consuming. Scientists are always searching for better methods of producing vaccines and for ways to develop vaccines for diseases with no effective vaccines. Many believe that genetic engineering holds the answer.

## Genetically Engineered Vaccines

The first vaccine using recombinant DNA technology was developed for the hepatitis B virus. To make this vaccine, researchers paste hepatitis B genes that code for the virus's antigens into yeast cells. The yeast cells multiply, producing antigens, and then scientists collect and purify the antigens to make a vaccine. Developing a vaccine for other diseases has been more difficult. Researchers have not yet successfully developed any other genetically engineered vaccines, but they are working on such vaccines for several different diseases, such as rabies, measles, and HIV.

HIV is the virus that causes AIDS. This virus can mutate so easily and has so many varied DNA sequences that finding antigens to use in a vaccine is tremendously challenging. In addition, its ability to mutate means that a vaccine that has been weakened or killed might turn infectious again when introduced into a person's body. No scientist would risk giving a person AIDS with a traditionally made vaccine. Nevertheless, in 2017 one research team, led by researcher Chil-Yong Kang of Western University in Canada, was conducting human trials with a genetically engineered and safe HIV vaccine. Kang and his team made the vaccine by first killing the virus and then using genetic engineering to make it safe. They removed some of the HIV genes and replaced them with genetic material from honeybees, making the coding instructions for entering and taking over human cells weak and ineffective. The first test of the vaccine (called a phase I trial) with a small group of volunteers showed that the vaccine was safe. No one got sick, and even though the virus was genetically modified, the volunteers' immune systems recognized it as foreign and made antibodies against it. No one knows yet if the immune response will be strong enough to protect people from AIDS. In the phase II trial, six hundred people will be given the vaccine to test its effectiveness. Kang and his team are hopeful. Kang says, "If we can show that this vaccine is effective in preventing people from contracting HIV, we can stop the AIDS epidemic and that would be tremendous. It would be a tremendous contribution to humankind, and it would make all of our efforts worthwhile."[26]

## Immunotherapy and Cancer

Vaccines activate the body's immune system in response to a threat, but a cancer treatment called CAR-T gene therapy uses a virus to change the genetic instructions in T cells and teach them to recognize and kill cancer cells. This treatment method has had some spectacular successes against acute lymphocytic leukemia (ALL). ALL is a cancer of white blood cells. Because of faulty coding instructions, the stem cells in the bone marrow, where blood cells are made, do not develop into the healthy white blood cells called B cells. Instead, the B cells produced are immature and multiply out of control. This is what happened to Ava Christianson. She was diagnosed with ALL in 2012 when she was four years old. Standard chemotherapy to kill cancer cells works to cure children with ALL about 90 percent of the time, but Ava was one of the 10 percent who relapsed; her cancer kept coming back. In 2016, when Ava was eight, her parents and doctors decided to try an experimental treatment to save her life.

**stem cells**

the body's master cells, capable of specializing into a variety of other cells to repair and replace damaged organs and tissues; the cells from which all other cells arise

# How CAR-T Gene Therapy Works

CAR-T gene therapy has had remarkable success in treating some forms of cancer. This therapy uses a virus to change the genetic instructions in T cells and teach them to recognize and kill cancer cells. To begin this therapy, a blood sample is drawn from the patient, and the T cells in the blood are separated out in the lab. The extracted T cells are infected with a virus that has been genetically engineered to carry the coding instructions for recognizing the cancerous cells. The genetically altered T cells are grown in the lab until there are millions of them that are then injected back into the patient's body. Once a part of the body's immune system, the CAR-T cells recognize the antigens of the cancerous cells and attack and kill them.

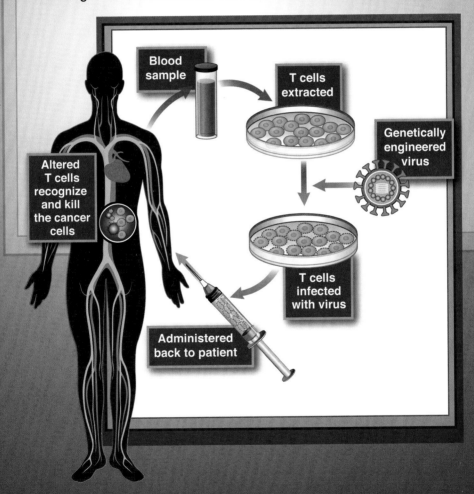

Source: Leukemia & Lymphoma Society, "Chimeric Antigen Receptor (CAR) T-Cell Therapy." www.lls.org/treatment/types-of-treatment/immunotherapy/chimeric-antigen-receptor-car-t-cell-therapy.

The treatment is called immunotherapy, because it boosts the immune system to fight disease. First, doctors acquired some of Ava's T cells from her blood. The T cells were extracted and then infected with a virus that was genetically altered to recognize the antigens on cancerous B cells. The cancer-recognizing T cells were multiplied in the lab until doctors had 30 million of them to inject back into Ava's body. There the T cells multiplied and began attacking her B cells. Ava's immune system response was powerful; her T cells attacked the cancer cells so fiercely that the child developed a fever of 106°F (41°C). Such a response is one danger of CAR-T gene therapy, but Ava's illness was brief. She recovered, her cancer disappeared, and as of 2017 doctors say she is in remission.

## Can Genetic Engineering Cure?

Dr. Terry Fry is the researcher in charge of the trial of CAR-T therapy at the National Cancer Institute, where Ava was treated. He is hopeful for a cure for Ava and everyone in his ex-

## Will Immunotherapy Be the Cancer Cure?

CAR-T cell therapy has been amazingly successful with the leukemia known as ALL, but the general strategy of engineering T cells to fight cancer might be applied to many kinds of cancer in the future. Researchers have already used CAR-T with small groups of patients to treat multiple myeloma (a cancer of blood plasma cells) and some kinds of lymphoma (a cancer of the lymph nodes). It has also been effective for adult patients with leukemia and other blood cancers. However, this immunotherapy does have limitations. Some trials of CAR-T have identified severe side effects. People developed extremely high fevers and other symptoms as their T cells responded too strongly to the cancer cells. In trials conducted by one research company, a few people died when their brains swelled for unknown reasons. Although no deaths have happened in trials by other research teams, all researchers are working to make the treatment safer.

CAR-T has been wonderfully effective with blood cancers, but the solid tumors of other kinds of cancer are harder to treat. Solid tumors are very good at suppressing the immune system, and T cells do not enter them well. Researchers are trying to figure out how to bring CAR-T therapy to bear on these forms of cancers, but so far they have not developed the technology to try the treatment in people. CAR-T is not yet the miracle cancer cure that scientists hope for, but researchers are rapidly working to bring it to its full potential.

perimental treatment study, but he is unsure if Ava will remain cancer free. He says, "I can't say that's going to be the case because we just don't know. It's too soon."[27] Nevertheless, 80 percent of patients in the trial achieved complete remission of their cancer.

In August 2017, because of the successful experimental trials, the FDA approved CAR-T therapy as a treatment for ALL when standard treatments have failed. It is the first gene therapy treatment to be approved in the United States. As other treatments are developed through genetic engineering, medical researchers predict that CAR-T therapy will be the first of many gene therapy treatments for cancer and that breakthrough treatments are coming in the near future for previously untreatable diseases.

# CHAPTER 4

# Gene Therapy and Genetic Diseases

Corey Haas was born with a rare, inherited genetic disorder called Leber's congenital amaurosis type 2 (LCA2). His disease was caused by a mutated gene that affected how his eyes worked. The layer of cells around his photoreceptors (rods and cones that capture light) did not store and process the vitamin A that nourishes the photoreceptors. As a result, Corey's rods and cones were gradually starving and dying. As an adult, he would become completely blind, but even as a child, Corey already saw only dark, blurred images and vague shapes. He bumped into things and could stare at a bright lightbulb and see just a faint, pale glow. Then in 2008, when Corey was eight years old, he received a new experimental gene therapy treatment. Doctors at Children's Hospital of Philadelphia injected 48 billion viruses containing healthy genes into the malfunctioning cell layer in Corey's left eye. Four days later Corey and his parents visited the Philadelphia Zoo. Over the entrance hung a huge, brightly colored balloon, and as Corey looked up into the strong sunshine to try to see the shape, something remarkable happened. He screamed, "The light! It hurts!"[28] and ducked and covered his eyes with his hands. Corey was frightened by a unique experience: He could see.

## From Mutated Genes to Healthy Genes

Gene therapy involves transplanting normal, healthy genes in order to replace, augment, or alter the abnormal, faulty genes that cause disease. Its fundamental goal is a one-time treatment that cures the disease by fixing the true problem—the mutated gene.

Writing for the *MIT Technology Review*, Antonio Regalado explains, "The dream of gene therapy is to fix your DNA so you're not sick anymore—a 'cure.'"[29] For the most part, gene therapy is still in its experimental stages. The technology is still being worked out, but the theory is well understood, and in some cases treatment seems to be amazingly successful. For people like Corey, born with rare single-gene inherited disorders, gene therapy holds great promise.

**congenital**

present from birth; inborn

Corey's treatment is a good example of how gene therapy works. His disease was caused by a mutation in the gene labeled RPE65. The story of identifying his mutated gene and then developing a therapy actually begins with briard dogs. This dog

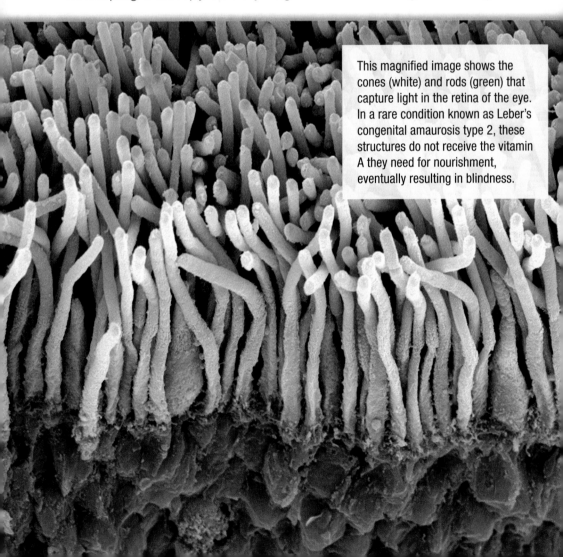

This magnified image shows the cones (white) and rods (green) that capture light in the retina of the eye. In a rare condition known as Leber's congenital amaurosis type 2, these structures do not receive the vitamin A they need for nourishment, eventually resulting in blindness.

breed carries a recessive gene mutation that causes a dog form of Leber's congenital amaurosis (LCA) and blindness, almost the same as in people. By breeding together dogs with LCA, researchers had a population of blind puppies in which to learn about the disease in detail. The precise fault in the gene was discovered in 1998; four bases in a row of the DNA in the RPE65 gene were missing. If scientists could replace that malfunctioning gene with a healthy one, perhaps the missing protein that coded for using vitamin A to feed the photoreceptors would be produced.

## A Viral Vector for Lancelot

The first problem was finding a delivery system for the healthy gene. The researchers chose an adeno-associated virus (AAV) to be the vector—or carrier—of the gene. AAV can infect humans and some primates, but it has never been known to cause disease. The immune system does not react to AAV. Researchers discovered that the virus could infect the eyes of the dogs, too. The second step was to remove two genes from the AAV and replace them with one healthy RPE65 gene derived from human cells, and a piece of DNA that helps regulate the gene. This is recombinant DNA technology similar to the process of making bacteria produce human insulin. Once the virus had multiplied billions of times in the laboratory, the scientists had to learn through a series of experiments with mice how much of the viral vectors to place in the dogs' eyes and how much to dilute the gene-carrying viruses before placing them in the eyes. Finally, the scientists were ready for the gene-transfer therapy that they hoped would restore vision to the dogs. If all went well, some of the cells would take up the correct coding instructions, function as healthy vitamin A–using cells, and nourish the photoreceptors that were starving and nonfunctional. Dr. William W. Hauswirth, one of the researchers who developed this gene-transfer thera-

> **vector**
>
> in medicine, a carrier of a disease, a medicine, or DNA; a mosquito is a vector of the malaria parasite, and a virus can be a vector when used to transfer a healthy gene into a human cell

py, explains, "The idea of gene transfer therapy is not rocket science, it's very simple. We're just treating these patients that are missing this function by supplying a normal copy, a good copy of the gene that they can use. . . . [We] put it inside the vector and target it to the right place surgically. The actual injection takes seconds."[30]

The first dog to receive the treatment was a blind puppy named Lancelot, who was treated in one eye in 2000. (In this first stage of experimentation, only one eye was treated. The second eye would be treated at a later time.) Jean Bennett, one of the doctors who would treat Corey eight years later, remembers how Lancelot behaved before his treatment. She says, "He'd bump into doors, and he couldn't find his water bowl. He became very timid and

## Gene Therapy for the Fertilized Egg

About one in every five thousand people has a mitochondrial genetic disease. Mitochondria are the powerhouses of the cell, providing its energy. Almost all a cell's genes are in the nucleus, but thirty-seven are in the mitochondria, outside the nucleus. If one of those genes mutates, the mitochondria do not work properly, resulting in severe disability for which there is no treatment. Mitochondrial disorders are passed from mother to offspring in the egg cells.

Researchers are trying to prevent these disorders with a technique called mitochondrial replacement therapy. With this technology, a doctor removes an egg from a woman's body and fertilizes it with the father's sperm in a laboratory dish—a process called in vitro fertilization. The nucleus of the fertilized egg is then removed from its cell and placed in a donor egg that has healthy mitochondria but its nucleus removed. The egg is placed back in the mother's uterus to develop into a healthy baby with no mitochondrial disease. That baby has 99.9 percent of the DNA inherited from its parents, but 0.1 percent of the DNA is from the donated egg. That means an individual has DNA from three people, an idea that disturbs many people. Mitochondrial replacement therapy is not allowed in the United States. In 2017 a baby was born when a New York team performed the procedure in Mexico. Another infant was born in China. The babies seem healthy, but many medical researchers worry about the long-term ramifications of altering DNA like this.

just sat there."[31] After his surgery, it did not take long for Lancelot to begin acting very differently. In just a few days, Lancelot and two other dogs who received the gene transfer started spinning in the lab. The dogs were so excited to see something out of one eye that they kept spinning around, almost dancing, to see as much of their world as they could. Bennett recalls, "At two months, Lancelot could see. When we saw the dramatic results, we knew we wanted to do it on humans."[32]

## Corey's Turn

None of the researchers were sure that the effects of the gene therapy would last, but when it came time for Corey's surgery, Lancelot and the other treated dogs were still seeing as well as ever. On September 25, 2008, Corey's ophthalmologist inserted 48 billion AAVs carrying a normal copy of RPE65 into the layer of cells around the photoreceptors of his left eye. As with the dogs, doctors treated only one eye for safety reasons. (In later years, Corey had his right eye treated, as well.) Some of the cells in Corey's left eye took up the virus and began coding for turning vitamin A into the form that his photoreceptors could use. At that time, a few young adults with LCA2 had been treated before, but Corey was the youngest person to undergo the procedure. It had worked spectacularly well for those young adults, and it did the same for Corey. Seeing the bright sunshine for the first time was only the beginning. As months passed, more and more of Corey's photoreceptors responded to the gene transfer.

**ophthalmologist**

a medical specialist in the treatment of diseases and disorders of the eye

In October, while Corey and his father were raking leaves outside, his father noticed something surprising. Cory's pupils had always been widely dilated, as his eyes struggled to take in all the light they could. Now his eyes were normally constricted—both eyes. Although the normal genes had remained in Corey's left eye where they were placed, the normal protein made by the genes had spread, even into the untreated eye. Some photoreceptors in Corey's right eye were being nourished, too. The same thing had happened with Lancelot and the other dogs. The restored vision was small, but a great benefit nonetheless. By the time he was ten years old, Corey still was nearsighted and had to wear thick glasses, but he could work on his computer, read an e-book, play baseball, and go out with his friends in the neighborhood at twilight.

No one with LCA2 has achieved 100 percent recovery of vision. The normal, working genes do not enter every cell that needs to be corrected; they are able to infect only the cells exactly where they were placed. In addition, LCA2 causes complete blindness because as the photoreceptors slowly starve, they shrivel and die. Nothing can regrow dead photoreceptors. However, in children like Corey, many photoreceptors are still alive. Geneticist Ricki Lewis explains, "That's why the younger a person is treated, the better—there's more to save."[33] In 2016 Corey turned sixteen, and his continuing functional vision allows him to live a normal life. Corey's mother says, "Corey worked this summer for the town of Hadley . . . grounds keeping, so he got to pick up the town parks, cut brush and clean up at the town garage."[34] Meanwhile, trials of LCA2 gene therapy continue, with researchers now treating both eyes of patients at the same time. The process continues to be safe, and 93 percent of patients have experienced an average improvement of two hundred times their initial level of vision. Researchers applied for FDA approval in 2017. It would be the first-ever approved gene therapy for a genetic disease in the United States.

## The Long Road to Success

In some ways gene therapy for blindness is an easier treatment than for other genetic disorders. The eye is like a closed system in the body; therefore, no vectors with genes can escape to other organs. In addition, the immune system remains outside the eye so no attacks on the foreign viruses are possible. Gene therapies used on other bodily systems can have unexpected and sometimes tragic results. In 1999 Jesse Gelsinger, for instance, died when he underwent a gene therapy trial using an adenovirus (AV) as a vector to deliver normal genes to an artery in his liver.

Eighteen-year-old Gelsinger suffered from a genetic condition known as ornithine transcarbamylase (OTC) deficiency. The disease meant that his body could not process the protein he ate. He had

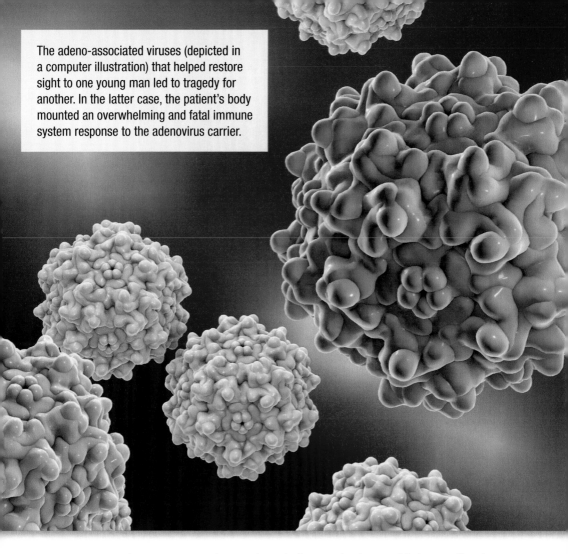

The adeno-associated viruses (depicted in a computer illustration) that helped restore sight to one young man led to tragedy for another. In the latter case, the patient's body mounted an overwhelming and fatal immune system response to the adenovirus carrier.

to remain on a severely restricted diet and take multiple medications to stay healthy. Gene therapy using an AV carrier was supposed to give him the normal genes that would enable his liver to process protein, but the experimental treatment did not turn out that way. Gelsinger's immune system mounted an overwhelming attack, even though the adenovirus (which normally is a cause of the common cold) had been altered to be safe. All of his body organs were affected, and there was nothing doctors could do to save him. It was not the altered genes that killed Gelsinger; it was the virus vector.

Scientists learned from Gelsinger's death to search for safer viral vectors (like AAV) and to be much more careful in their research before trying gene therapy on people. New gene transfer treatments are studied for fifteen years or more in trials and tests, but hundreds of such gene therapy trials are ongoing throughout the world. Even though single-gene diseases are rare diseases, there are more than five thousand of them, and that means thousands of people for whom gene therapy may be the only answer.

## Gene Therapy for Stem Cells

OTC deficiency and LCA2 are both rare diseases caused by a recessive mutated gene, but one of the rarest diseases in the world is adenosine deaminase severe combined immunodeficiency (ADA-SCID), sometimes called "bubble boy" disease. It is a genetic disorder that deprives children of a functioning immune system. It is estimated that only about fourteen children a year are born with ADA-SCID in Europe and another twelve in the United States. These children would die of infection soon after birth unless kept in sterile conditions. Gene therapy seems to be curing these children by correcting the genetic instructions in the stem cells in the bone marrow, where immune system white blood cells are grown.

Stem cells are the body's master cells; they can specialize and grow into many different kinds of cells. The stem cells in the bone marrow are constantly making new blood cells, including those of the immune system. To correct ADA-SCID, researchers at the drug company GlaxoSmithKline developed a genetic treatment named Strimvelis. Strimvelis is a technology that involves removing some stem cells from a patient's bone marrow, soaking them in viruses carrying a correct copy of the mutated gene that causes ADA-SCID, and then growing the stem cells carrying the normal gene in the lab. The stem cell solution is then purified to remove any stray viruses and injected back into the patient's bone marrow. There the now-normal stem cells specialize into normal immune cells that protect against disease. Every cell specialized from the stem cells carries normal genetic instructions. This treatment has been used for at least fifteen years with children with ADA-SCID. Of the eighteen children treated, all are still alive, none had any adverse reactions, and all are living normal lives. Strimvelis seems to be a permanent cure, but it will be many more years before scientists know with certainty whether treatment will ever be needed again. Nevertheless, Strimvelis was approved for use in Europe in 2016. Sven Kili, the head of gene therapy development at GlaxoSmithKline, says, "I would be hesitant to call it a cure, although there's no reason to think it won't last."[35]

## Hope for More Successes

GlaxoSmithKline is hoping to develop many more treatments for other rare diseases using its laboratory techniques, and eventually the researchers want to extend the technology for use with other genetic disorders. Kili explains, "If we can first make products that change lives, then we can develop them into things that affect more people. We believe gene therapy is an area of important future growth."[36] Other drug companies and researchers have the same goals. Some of the genetic diseases for which gene therapies are being tested include beta thalassemia, sickle cell disease, and hemophilia. Severe beta thalassemia is a kind

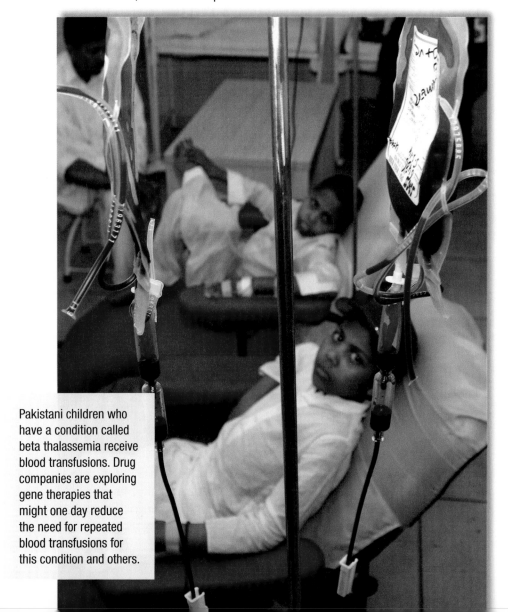

Pakistani children who have a condition called beta thalassemia receive blood transfusions. Drug companies are exploring gene therapies that might one day reduce the need for repeated blood transfusions for this condition and others.

# A Future with No Inherited Disease?

Someday, using a technique called gene editing, genetic mutations may be corrected before an embryo even begins to develop. In August 2017 an international team of researchers led by Oregon Health and Science University reported that they corrected a mutation in lab-grown embryos. The researchers used donated eggs, fertilized with sperm donated from men who carried the mutation, which causes a heart defect. At the same time that they fertilized the eggs, the researchers deleted the mutated gene, and the embryos used the mother's DNA to rewrite the DNA code.

The researchers employed a technique known as CRISPR-Cas9 gene editing. Cas9 is an enzyme (a kind of protein) that acts like scissors and cuts DNA at precise locations. The enzyme is guided with a bit of RNA called guide RNA that shows the enzyme where to cut. Thus, the mutated DNA in the gene is deleted, and as the embryo recognizes the damage and tries to repair it, corrected DNA replaces damaged DNA. The technology is a powerful but controversial tool that might eliminate many genetic disorders. Every cell in the developing fetus copies and carries the correction, including the egg or sperm that will pass the changes from generation to generation. In the 2017 study, the embryos were discarded. More research and ethical discussions are necessary before gene-edited embryos are implanted in women. Few people are comfortable with gene editing that changes human DNA for future generations, and no one yet knows all the risks that may be involved.

of anemia in which malfunctioning red blood cells do not deliver enough oxygen to the body. People born with this genetic disease depend on a lifetime of regular blood transfusions to survive. Sickle cell disease also often requires blood transfusions. In several successful trials of gene therapy for beta thalassemia and sickle cell disease, bone marrow stem cells that were corrected and transplanted using a viral vector have led to some people being able to stop blood transfusions and others reducing the number of blood transfusions needed by 60 percent. As of 2017 trials with these treatments were still ongoing.

In 2016 the gene therapy company Spark Therapeutics was able to announce that four people with hemophilia were being cured with gene therapy. At least, these people (who were missing the genetic instructions that code for blood being able to clot) had stopped having uncontrolled bleeding episodes. The protein that hemophiliacs are missing, factor IX, is manufactured in the liver. That means the viral vectors have to be taken up by the appropriate liver cells while escaping detection by the body's immune system. The four people seemingly cured of their hemophilia averaged only 30 percent of normal factor IX in their cells, but that is enough to prevent abnormal bleeding from minor injuries. No one knows if the effects of the genetic treatment will last or if it will work for most people with hemophilia. Spark is a company established by Katherine High, a researcher at Children's Hospital of Philadelphia who is also working on gene therapy for LCA2. High explains, "This is four subjects. We are going to need more. If you saw that in 40 subjects, then maybe . . . well, it's very exciting."[37]

Studies for gene therapy for hemophilia are ongoing and do face a problem. The viral vector causes an immune system reaction in 40 percent of people because they have previously been infected by the virus naturally and have developed antibodies against it. The reaction is not dangerous, but it does mean that the viruses and the corrected cells they infect are killed by the immune system, so the effects of the treatment do not last for those people. High and the other Spark scientists are working to overcome this problem, but they are extremely encouraged by their ongoing research. Even 60 percent of hemophiliacs is an exciting number to think of when they may be talking about a permanent cure.

## The Ultimate Goal

The ultimate goal for researchers is a gene therapy strategy that will successfully address all the genetic diseases by delivering healthy, normal genes to the right place in each individual who needs them. Ricki Lewis believes that gene therapies for many diseases will explode in the near future. She explains, "It is the only way to correct the biochemical instructions that make us sick. Gene therapy will be a forever fix."[38] Someday, it may be medicine's ultimate solution.

# CHAPTER 5

# Prenatal Genetic Testing

Laura (full name withheld for privacy) was thirty-three years old and pregnant with her third child. Even though her first two children were normal and healthy, she had had a miscarriage in the eighteenth week of her previous pregnancy. This time, she wanted some reassurance that her developing baby was healthy. She told her doctor, "I would like to get this all wrapped up and know the pregnancy is okay."[39] Laura underwent a procedure called chorionic villus sampling (CVS). Her doctor inserted a needle into her uterus to draw off some placental cells. The placenta is the organ in the uterus that provides nourishment for the developing fetus. The chorionic villi are wispy, fingerlike projections from the placenta that share genetic material with the fetus. Laura's cell sample was analyzed in the laboratory under a microscope for evidence of any abnormal chromosomes. Further DNA testing also can be done to search for some specific genetic disorders, such as Tay-Sachs disease or CF. Laura was able to have CVS in the first trimester (first three months) of her pregnancy. The procedure provided her peace of mind that the fetus was developing normally.

## Amniocentesis: The First Prenatal Test

The ability to diagnose the health of a fetus is relatively new. During the 1960s scientists developed such prenatal testing to identify chromosome abnormalities, but the procedure—known as amniocentesis—was used only with mothers at high risk of giving birth to a child with a birth defect. For example, mothers older than thirty-five are at higher risk of having a baby with Down syndrome than are younger mothers. Down syndrome is also called trisomy 21, because affected individuals have an extra copy of chromosome 21. This error can cause developmen-

| | |
|---|---|
| **placenta** | |
| the circular, flattish organ in the uterus that nourishes the growing baby through the umbilical cord | |

tal delays and intellectual and physical disabilities. In the United States about six thousand babies with Down syndrome are born each year. Amniocentesis is performed during the second trimester (fifteen to twenty weeks into the pregnancy). It involves withdrawing some of the amniotic fluid that surrounds the developing baby by puncturing a thin needle into the uterus through the mother's abdominal wall. Some of the fetal cells fall into the amniotic fluid, and these cells can be tested in the laboratory for damaged chromosomes.

Damaged or extra chromosomes generally occur because of errors that happen as a fertilized egg develops into an embryo and then a fetus. Chromosomal abnormalities usually are not inherited disorders but genetic mistakes in development. Any chromosome pair can have an extra copy, or trisomy, but most such disorders are not compatible with life, and the fetus dies and is miscarried early in the pregnancy. However, other trisomies that can lead to disability may result in a live birth. Trisomy 13 and trisomy 18, for example, cause severe physical defects, and most infants born with the disorders die within the first few days or months of life. Since chromosomes are large and easy to see in the lab, these chromosomal disorders, as well as trisomy 21, can be diagnosed with close to 100 percent certainty with amniocentesis.

| | |
|---|---|
| **amniotic fluid** | |
| the clear, slightly yellow fluid surrounding a developing fetus in the amniotic sac | |

## Amniocentesis Today

For many years amniocentesis was quite expensive and could be dangerous for the fetus, perhaps causing a miscarriage. It was offered to very few women, but today the procedure is economical and safe, with a miscarriage risk of only about 0.5 percent. It is offered to any pregnant woman, but commonly, the women who choose to have it done are over thirty-five or know that they have an increased risk of having a baby with a genetic abnormality. Since about 1997 doctors have been able to use amniocentesis to diagnose more than eight hundred different inherited disorders. Genetic disorders can be diagnosed through DNA analysis of the fetal cells in the amniotic fluid. Genetic analysis takes longer than chromosomal analysis, which takes a few days. Identification of genetic disorders generally takes about two or three weeks.

Amniocentesis is also used as a diagnostic tool for neural tube defects, such as spina bifida. Spina bifida is a condition in which the spinal cord does not develop normally and may have an opening where the spinal cord pokes through the spine. Neural tube

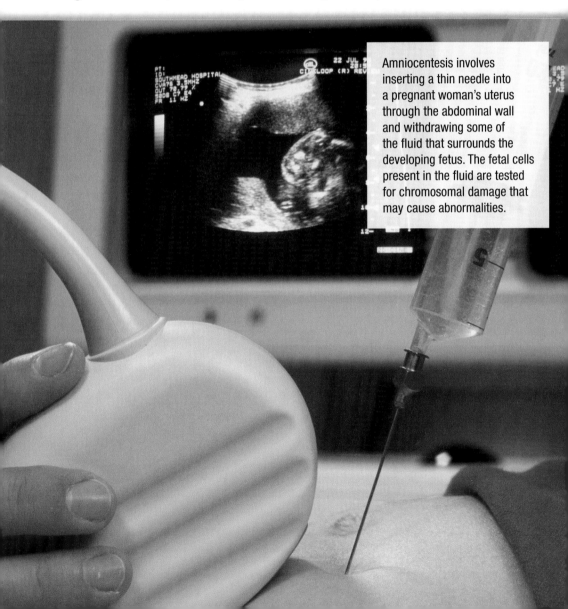

Amniocentesis involves inserting a thin needle into a pregnant woman's uterus through the abdominal wall and withdrawing some of the fluid that surrounds the developing fetus. The fetal cells present in the fluid are tested for chromosomal damage that may cause abnormalities.

defects, in general, are defects in the brain or spinal cord. They may be indicated when a substance produced by the fetus called alpha-fetoprotein appears in the amniotic fluid in high amounts.

Amniocentesis is an extremely valuable prenatal testing technology, but there are disadvantages. First, it is an invasive procedure, meaning the woman's abdominal wall and uterus are punctured by the needle used to draw off the fluid. Although the risk of hitting the fetus with the needle or causing a miscarriage is very small, such accidents can occur. And as with any invasive procedure, there is a slight risk of infection in the mother. In addition, for safety reasons, amniocentesis is almost always performed during the fifteenth to twentieth weeks of pregnancy. This means that the fetus is already four or five months old, and the parents have had to wait a long time into the pregnancy before finding out if the unborn child is healthy.

The biggest issue with amniocentesis is an ethical one for many people. If, for example, the test results indicate that the

## Newborn Testing

In the United States and many other modern countries, all newborns are screened for congenital disorders and conditions. Generally, a small sample of the baby's blood is drawn from the heel and sent to a state laboratory for analysis. The vast majority of babies test as perfectly healthy, but early detection of congenital problems results in the ability to treat infants before they get sick. One important test is for phenylketonuria (PKU), which prevents individuals from properly digesting proteins. Untreated, PKU can cause severe mental and physical disabilities, but when diagnosed at birth, a special diet and medication prevent disabilities from developing.

Today modern hospitals routinely test for approximately twenty-nine major disorders, including ADA-SCID, CF, sickle cell disease, galactosemia, and congenital hypothyroidism. If a baby tests positive for congenital hypothyroidism, for instance, he or she has little or no thyroid gland function and may become severely disabled. But with treatment begun in the first two weeks of life, such a child can develop normally. A newborn with galactosemia cannot digest milk and will develop serious illnesses and ultimately die unless given a special diet from birth. Even if the condition found is not completely treatable, as is true with CF, newborn screening is valuable. The earlier a child with CF begins a special diet, is guarded against germs, and receives treatments to keep the lungs clear, the healthier the child will be for years to come.

infant will be born with Down syndrome or CF, the parents must decide what to do with this information. Some people use the knowledge to prepare themselves for the birth of a child with a disorder or to choose a specialized hospital for the birth so as to have the best medical care available for the child. Most often, however, the information is used to decide whether to terminate the pregnancy (have an abortion). For many people, this is an agonizing moral decision. They wonder if it is right to terminate a pregnancy because the child will have a defect. They ask whether individuals born with a disorder such as Down syndrome or CF can live happy, worthwhile, and fulfilling lives just as much as an unimpaired baby can. Even people who do not completely reject the idea of an abortion can have concerns. Writing for the *Princeton Journal of Bioethics*, Rucha Alur explains, "Lastly, the amniocentesis test is administered very late in the pregnancy, during the second trimester. At this point the fetus is already the size of an apple and has been moving for a couple weeks. Since abortion is legal in most states until viability, these abortions are still technically allowed but some consider them to be past the point of an ethical abortion."[40]

> **miscarriage**
>
> the expulsion of a fetus from the uterus before the twentieth week of pregnancy and thus before the fetus can survive independently

## The Sooner the Better

Medical researchers developed CVS, the procedure Laura had, during the 1980s, hoping to address some of the problems with amniocentesis—particularly diagnosing problems earlier in the pregnancy. Although CVS is still an invasive procedure, the fact that it can be performed safely between ten and thirteen weeks of pregnancy is a distinct advantage. Should the test reveal a chromosomal abnormality like Down syndrome, the parents may find it easier to decide to terminate the pregnancy at this earlier stage of fetal development. For the vast majority of women such as Laura, the results offer the reassurance that the baby will be healthy. A disadvantage of CVS is that it cannot detect neural tube defects. It also carries a slightly higher risk of miscarriage than amniocentesis, but the risk is still a little less than 1 percent.

By 2011 noninvasive screening tests made CVS and amniocentesis unnecessary for many women who want to know if a fetus has a genetic abnormality. Simple maternal blood tests, taken from the mother at about ten weeks into the pregnancy, can now identify trisomies and some genetic problems in the fetus. This is possible because DNA from the fetus and placenta circulates in the mother's blood from the beginning of the pregnancy. The DNA is cell-free DNA. It is not inside the nuclei of cells but floating freely in the mother's bloodstream. In the laboratory, maternal DNA can be separated from fetal DNA, which is then examined for abnormalities. A maternal blood test used for assessing the fetus is called noninvasive prenatal testing (NIPT). NIPT is almost as accurate at finding chromosomal defects as CVS or amniocentesis. Down syndrome, for example, is detected 99 percent of the time. However, blood tests are still only screening tests, not diagnostic tests. Screening tests indicate an increased risk of a fetal abnormality, but an actual diagnosis that the abnormality is there for sure depends on a diagnostic test like amniocentesis. Screening tests inform doctors and patients that the more invasive diagnostic test is necessary.

## Modern Screening Problems

Screening tests, however, have limitations. When used to identify genetic abnormalities other than trisomies, their accuracy rates may be only about 80 percent, meaning they may fail to pick up a genetic disorder 20 percent of the time. An even larger problem is that the tests may indicate an abnormality when there is none, a situation that is called a false positive. NIPT yields a lot of false positive results. Up to 50 percent of positive results for Down syndrome, for example, are false positives. The testing rarely misses the fact that the fetus has Down syndrome when it does, but it indicates a problem when the baby does not have Down syndrome almost half the time. False positives are high for tri-

**false positive**

an incorrect test result that indicates a condition is present when it is not

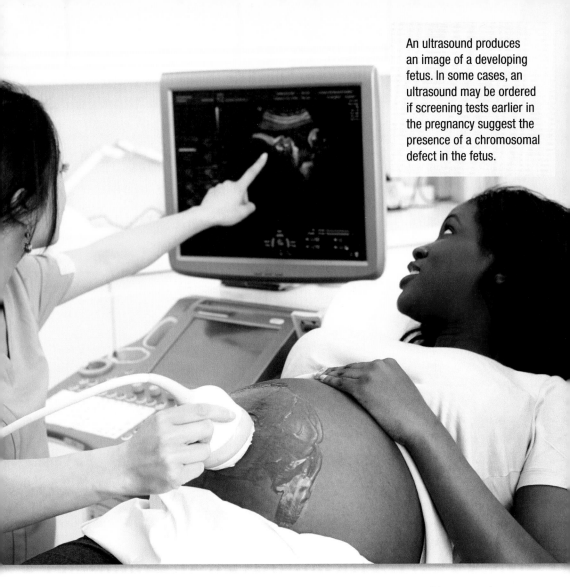

An ultrasound produces an image of a developing fetus. In some cases, an ultrasound may be ordered if screening tests earlier in the pregnancy suggest the presence of a chromosomal defect in the fetus.

somy 13 and trisomy 18, too. This means that any positive result must be evaluated later in the pregnancy, either with an invasive prenatal test or an ultrasound (a medical imaging technique to examine the fetus).

For parents who are informed of a positive screening result, waiting for a diagnostic test can be terrifying. Zachary Diamond, for example, remembers when his wife, Angie Nunes, had NIPT and the results came back positive for trisomy 18. Diamond says, "If you google Trisomy 18, your heart will just shatter with the prognosis [predicted outcome]. The prognosis is godless, just awful. Angie was crying on the sofa for hours on end."[41] As it turned out, the result was a false positive, and the baby was born

## Prepregnancy Genetic Testing

Some couples, especially from certain populations or from families with a history of genetic disorders, choose to undergo genetic testing before becoming pregnant. In this way the prospective parents can discover if either is a carrier of a recessive genetic disorder and determine the risk to any future children. Some genetic medical specialists believe that this carrier screening should be offered to all prospective parents. If parents determine that they are carriers of a genetic disorder, they can choose not to have children, choose adoption, opt for in vitro fertilization techniques so as to select a healthy embryo to be implanted in the mother, or decide whether the risk to the future child is reasonable.

The decision is often based on the severity of the disorder. Tay-Sachs disease, for example, is an autosomal recessive disorder that occurs most frequently in the Jewish population originating in eastern Europe. If both parents are carriers of the Tay-Sachs gene, each pregnancy has a 25 percent risk of a baby with Tay-Sachs—a progressive disorder that is always fatal in the first two or three years of life. Through carrier screening offered to Jewish populations in modern countries, Jewish communities have reduced the incidence of Tay-Sachs births in the United States and Canada by 95 percent. Anyone can carry the Tay-Sachs gene, but it is very rare in other ethnic groups. The effort among Jewish communities has been a true success story in the use of genetic screening to almost eliminate a deadly disease.

perfectly healthy. But the parents did not know that the baby was fine until Nunes was sixteen weeks pregnant and could have an ultrasound. Many doctors and parents alike wonder if the fear and grief they go through before a fetus can be accurately diagnosed is justified. They wonder about the value of screening tests and also worry that such false positives are causing unnecessary abortions.

Stacie Chapman of Tiverton, Rhode Island, almost terminated her pregnancy when her NIPT came back positive for trisomy 18 early in her pregnancy. When she received the results, she scheduled an abortion for the next day. Then her doctor called her and talked to her about false positives. He urged her to wait until she could have a diagnostic test at twenty weeks into her pregnancy. Chapman agreed, and the later testing showed that the baby was normal—but she could not forget the possibility that her child might be born with a fatal disorder. She recalls now, "The rest of the pregnancy was traumatic and it didn't have to be this way. I tried not to bond with the baby and didn't want to talk to anyone about it or tell people at work. I didn't even want to have a baby shower."[42] Not until her son was born perfectly normal was the worried mother able to relax.

Some studies have suggested that fetuses are sometimes aborted due to screening tests alone, despite expert medical recommendations that parents be counseled about the shortcomings and limitations of NIPT. No one knows if this means that some healthy fetuses are aborted because of too much reliance on the test results. Other people—parents, genetic counselors, medical researchers, and experts in medical ethics— also worry about the moral issues connected with NIPT. In 2015 the United Nations Educational, Scientific and Cultural Organization issued a report saying of NIPT, "[It means] indirectly that certain lives are worth living, and others less."[43] Advocates for people with Down syndrome are especially disturbed by early screening for trisomy 21, because they say that people with Down syndrome deserve to be valued and not eliminated from society. Yet often, a fetus diagnosed with Down syndrome is aborted.

## Concerns over Prenatal Testing

One 2015 study estimates that since prenatal testing has become a reality, the population of people with Down syndrome in the United States has been reduced by 30 percent. In Europe and the United Kingdom, it is estimated that 53 percent of Down syndrome pregnancies are terminated. Other studies have suggested that when Down syndrome is diagnosed prenatally, up to 90 percent of the pregnancies are terminated. In Iceland, which has nationwide prenatal testing, Down syndrome has almost completely disappeared from the population. Only one or two affected babies are born each year because almost 100 percent of parents terminate the pregnancy when prenatal testing is positive for Down syndrome.

Mark Bradford is president of the Jérôme Lejeune Foundation USA, an organization devoted to advocacy for those with intelligence disorders. He argues that

> the only thing prenatal diagnosis can provide is a first impression of who a child will be. Making such a radical decision as to end the life of a child based upon a first impression is a most horrible and violent form of discrimination. It has no place in an American society that is committed to ending discrimination in any form and that has intensified that effort for persons with disabilities over the last 25 years since the signing of the Americans with Disabilities Act in July 1990.[44]

Many in the medical community see great benefit to prenatal testing, especially when done early. However, as the ability to detect more and more genetic variables improves, ethical questions

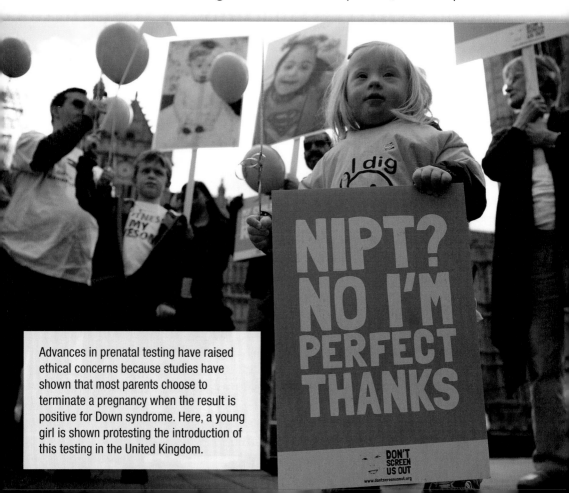

Advances in prenatal testing have raised ethical concerns because studies have shown that most parents choose to terminate a pregnancy when the result is positive for Down syndrome. Here, a young girl is shown protesting the introduction of this testing in the United Kingdom.

will continue to be raised. Dr. Ronald Wapner, an expert in fetal testing, asks, "What should we test a fetus for? I'm not suggesting at all that this is bad, but we need to have a discussion about where we are going with this ability. The technology is fantastic. But the easier it is to get information, the more tempted we may be to let our guard down on what we look for."[45] Already, prenatal testing can be used to identify more than just severe genetic disorders. It can determine the sex of the baby, and the entire fetal genome can be sequenced. In addition, researchers are rapidly learning which genes and gene variations and mutations determine which traits. Soon, scientists predict, it will be possible to predict multiple individual characteristics by testing a six-week-old fetus. One research study, for example, discovered a tiny gene variation that increases the risk for nearsightedness or mild hearing loss. Perhaps increased risk of learning disabilities, depression, future heart disease, or tendency to obesity will be diagnosed with early prenatal testing. Perhaps the day will come when it is possible to eliminate all perceived genetic disadvantages, no matter how mild, from the human race by terminating undesirable pregnancies.

Many people wonder if prenatal genetic testing will lead to the birth of only "designer babies" who are perfect representatives of the child parents want. Emily Oster is a parent and economics professor who has thought at length about the implications of genetic testing. She says:

> In principle, this technology could be used to detect anything for which we have a known genetic link. . . . What if you could know, at six weeks of pregnancy, whether your child would inherit your height, or hair color, or IQ?. . . Many people terminate a pregnancy when they learn the fetus has Down Syndrome. What about learning that the child will have autism? Or simply that their IQ is likely to be below average? We are holding Pandora's box. Once we open it and let the information out, we lose control over what it is used for. . . . Ready or not, the future is coming.[46]

Despite the great benefits of genetic science, society has to figure out how to ensure that the technologies will be used for the good of all.

# SOURCE NOTES

## Introduction: A Revolution in Medicine
1. Quoted in Bob Tedeschi, "The Survivors: How an Experimental Treatment Saved Patients and Changed Medicine," STAT, April 25, 2017. www.statnews.com.
2. Quoted in Tedeschi, "The Survivors."
3. Quoted in Tedeschi, "The Survivors."
4. Quoted in Medical Xpress, "*New England Journal of Medicine* Publishes Long-Term Results of Gleevec for Patients with Chronic Myeloid Leukemia," March 9, 2017. https://medical xpress.com.
5. National Cancer Institute, "The Genetics of Cancer," May 1, 2017. www.cancer.gov.

## Chapter 1: Understanding Genes and DNA
6. Virtual Genetics Education Centre, "DNA, Genes, and Chromosomes." www2.le.ac.uk.
7. Barry Starr, "Dominant vs. Recessive: How Can 2 Parents with Dwarfism Have a Child That Is of Average Height?," Tech Museum of Innovation, Stanford School of Medicine, June 23, 2006. http://genetics.thetech.org.
8. Ricki Lewis, *The Forever Fix: Gene Therapy and the Boy Who Saved It*. New York: St. Martin's, 2012, p. 77.
9. Steven Monroe Lipkin with Jon Luoma, *The Age of Genomes: Tales from the Frontlines of Genetic Medicine*. Boston: Beacon, 2016, p. 5.
10. Jim Clark, "DNA—Mutations," Chemguide, May 2016. www .chemguide.co.uk.
11. National Institutes of Health, "Human Genome Project," March 29, 2013. https://report.nih.gov.

## Chapter 2: Personalized Medicine
12. Angelina Jolie, "My Medical Choice," *New York Times*, May 14, 2013. www.nytimes.com.

13. Angelina Jolie, "Angelina Jolie Pitt: Diary of a Surgery," *New York Times*, March 24, 2015. www.nytimes.com.
14. Quoted in Carolyn Y. Johnson, "The Unintended Consequence of Angelina Jolie's Viral Breast Cancer Essay," *Washington Post*, December 15, 2016. www.washingtonpost.com.
15. Quoted in Cystic Fibrosis Foundation, "FDA Approves Ivacaftor for 23 Additional CFTR Mutations," May 17, 2017. www.cff.org.
16. National Institutes of Health, "About the All of Us Research Program," 2017. https://allofus.nih.gov.
17. American Cancer Society, "How Does Breast Cancer Form?," About Breast Cancer, August 18, 2016. www.cancer.org.
18. Cancer Genome Atlas, "Impact of Cancer Genomics on Precision Medicine for the Treatment of Cancer." https://cancergenome.nih.gov.
19. Quoted in Diane Mapes, "Living with Stage 4," Fred Hutch News Service, October 13, 2016. www.fredhutch.org.
20. Quoted in Angelica Welch, "Expert Weighs In on Future of HER2-Positive Breast Cancer Treatment," OncLive, April 20, 2017. www.onclive.com.
21. Quoted in Linda Geddes, "Underfunded, Undertreated: Lung Cancer in Nonsmokers on the Rise," *Chicago Tribune*, August 22, 2012. http://articles.chicagotribune.com.
22. Quoted in Jeanne Erdmann, "How Personalized Medicine Is Changing: Lung Cancer," Genome. http://genomemag.com.

## Chapter 3: Creating New Medicines
23. Quoted in Arlene Weintraub, "FDA Panel Gives Thumbs-Up to Amgen's Virus-Based Melanoma Drug," *Forbes*, April 29, 2015. www.forbes.com.
24. Quoted in Carly Baldwin, "New Jersey Has Higher Rates of Melanoma than Other States," Woodbridge Patch, May 22, 2016. https://patch.com.
25. Quoted in Baldwin, "New Jersey Has Higher Rates of Melanoma than Other States."
26. Quoted in Fiona MacDonald, "A First-of-Its-Kind HIV Vaccine Will Move to Phase II Trials in 2017," ScienceAlert, December 5, 2016. www.sciencealert.com.
27. Quoted in Laurie McGinley, "This 8-Year-Old Is Free of Cancer—for Now—After a 'Breakthrough' Treatment," *Washington Post*, October 4, 2016. www.washingtonpost.com.

## Chapter 4: Gene Therapy and Genetic Diseases

28. Quoted in Lewis, *The Forever Fix*, p. x.
29. Antonio Regalado, "Everything You Need to Know About Gene Therapy's Most Promising Year," *MIT Technology Review*, December 30, 2016. www.technologyreview.com.
30. Quoted in Anita Manning, "Gene Therapy for Childhood Blindness," National Eye Institute. https://nei.nih.gov.
31. Quoted in Lewis, *The Forever Fix*, p. 245.
32. Quoted in Lewis, *The Forever Fix*, p. 246.
33. Lewis, *The Forever Fix*, p. 258.
34. Quoted in Ricki Lewis, "Three Gene Therapy Trials Report Good News," *DNA Science Blog*, PLOS, August 22, 2016. http://blogs.plos.org.
35. Quoted in Antonio Regalado, "Gene Therapy's First Out-and-Out Cure Is Here," *MIT Technology Review*, May 6, 2016. www.technologyreview.com.
36. Quoted in Regalado, "Gene Therapy's First Out-and-Out Cure Is Here."
37. Quoted in Antonio Regalado, "Gene Therapy Is Curing Hemophilia," *MIT Technology Review*, June 11, 2016. www.tech nologyreview.com.
38. Lewis, *The Forever Fix*, p. 303.

## Chapter 5: Prenatal Genetic Testing

39. Quoted in Bonnie Rochman, *The Gene Machine: How Genetic Technologies Are Changing the Way We Have Kids—and the Kids We Have*. New York: Scientific American, 2017. Kindle edition.
40. Rucha Alur, "The Controversy Behind an 'Amnio,'" *Princeton Journal of Bioethics*, April 27, 2017. https://pjb.mycpanel2 .princeton.edu.
41. Quoted in NBC News, "Prenatal Tests Have High Failure Rate, Triggering Abortions," December 14, 2014. www.nbcnews .com.
42. Quoted in NBC News, "Prenatal Tests Have High Failure Rate, Triggering Abortions."
43. Quoted in Stop Discriminating Down, "UNESCO Reports: Systematic Prenatal Screening Followed by an Abortion

Indirectly Means That Certain Lives Are Worth Living, and Others Less," February 21, 2017. https://stopdiscriminating down.com.

44. Mark Bradford, "New Study: Abortion After Prenatal Diagnosis of Down Syndrome Reduces Down Syndrome Community by Thirty Percent," Lozier Institute, April 21, 2015. https://lozierinstitute.org.

45. Quoted in Rochman, *The Gene Machine*.

46. Emily Oster, "Pandora's Baby: How a New Type of Prenatal Genetic Testing Could Predict Your Child," *Time*, 2017. http://time.com.

# FOR FURTHER RESEARCH

c

## Books

David Bond, *Genetic Engineering*. Broomall, PA: Mason Crest, 2017.

Fred Bortz, *The Laws of Genetics and Gregor Mendel*. New York: Rosen Classroom, 2014.

Petra Miller, *Cystic Fibrosis*. New York: Cavendish Square, 2016.

Petra Miller, *Down Syndrome*. New York: Cavendish Square, 2016.

Megan Mitchell, *The Human Genome*. New York: Cavendish Square, 2016.

James Wolfe, ed., *Genetic Testing and Gene Therapy*. New York: Rosen, 2015.

## Internet Sources

Ainsley Newson, "Why Should We Offer Screening for Down Syndrome Anyway?," Conversation, August 11, 2014. http://theconversation.com/why-should-we-offer-screening-for-down-syndrome-anyway-30351.

Rich Shea, "Curing Blindness, Part I: Corey's Story," *Eye on the Cure* (blog), Foundation Fighting Blindness, December 18, 2012. www.blindness.org/blog/index.php/curing-blindness-part-1-coreys-story.

Yourgenome.org, "Is Germline Gene Therapy Ethical?," Wellcome Genome Campus, June 3, 2015. https://www.yourgenome.org/debates/is-germline-gene-therapy-ethical.

## Websites

**Emily Whitehead Foundation** (http://emilywhiteheadfoundation .org). Whitehead was the first child to be cured of cancer with

d
e
f
g
h
i
j
k
l
m
n
o
p
q
r
s
t
u
v
w
x

CAR-T cell therapy. Her parents set up the foundation to support research into innovative cancer treatments and tell her story, as well as explain the therapy that saved her.

**Genetics Home Reference** (https://ghr.nlm.nih.gov). At this site from the NIH, visitors can explore the basics of genetics, the genetic causes of more than one thousand health conditions, and up-to-date articles about precision medicine and genetic screening of newborn infants.

**National Cancer Institute** (www.cancer.gov). Follow the links on this large website to learn what cancer is, how it develops, the genetics of cancer, and information about ongoing cancer clinical trials.

**Virtual Genetics Education Centre, University of Leicester** (www2.le.ac.uk/projects/vgec/geneticsall). This UK site provides easy-to-understand tutorials about DNA, genes, and chromosomes. It also has sections about gene therapy and ethical issues involving genetics.

# INDEX

# PICTURE CREDITS

Cover: iStockphoto.com

4: Shutterstock.com/Oksana Alekseeva (top)

4: Shutterstock/Jordan Lye (bottom left)

4: iStockphoto.com/Dr_Microbe (bottom right)

5: Shutterstock.com/Kateryna Kon

8: Steve Gschmeissner/Science Photo Library

12: Gregor Mendel (oil on canvas), Austrian school (19th century)/private collection/De Agostini Picture Library/ Bridgeman Images

16: Maury Aaseng

19: James King-Holmes/Science Source

23: Associated Press

27: PhotoStock-Israel/Science Source

32: Dennis Kunkel Microscopy/Science Source

35: National Cancer Institute/Science Photo Library

39: Ricardo Ramirez/KRT/Newscom

43: Maury Aaseng

47: Steve Gschmeissner/Science Source

52: Shutterstock.com/Kateryna Kon

54: Pacific Press/Sipa USA/Newscom

59: Saturn Stills/Science Photo Library

63: iStockphoto.com/monkeybusinessimages

66: Stefan Rousseau/Zuma Press/Newscom

Toney Allman holds degrees from Ohio State University and the University of Hawaii. She currently lives in Virginia, where she enjoys a rural lifestyle as well as researching and writing about a variety of topics for students.